SHELTER
FOR THE
SPIRITUALLY
HOMELESS

SHELTER
FOR THE
SPIRITUALLY
HOMELESS

Donna Schaper

St. Louis, Missouri

Cover Painting: Anne Croghan
Cover Design: Maria Cummins
Art Director: Michael Dominguez

1 2 3 4 5 6 7 8 9 10   99 98 97 96 95

Library of Congress Cataloging–in–Publication Data

(pending)

Printed in the United States of America

Contents

▮ INTRODUCTION

A stooped old woman trudges down the street. Her shopping bag contains everything she owns. Eventually she stops at a mound of abandoned cardboard boxes, rearranges them and moves in. Backing into her dwelling she catches the eye of someone observing her from across the street.

A well-dressed woman is hailing a cab and following the old woman's journey. *One journey is outer,* she thinks, *and one is inner. I hope as much as she does that something— anything—will happen. Anything but this life of a modern nomad, a plane circling, running out of fuel, no place to land, no country to call its own, no shelter from the irritation and the obligations and the anxiety. The cab passed me right by— and I have so much yet to do.*

Many of us in the American middle class are spiritually homeless. We have better roofs than the genuinely poor but not better foundations.

Across the way, the old woman unpacks her bag, takes off her ill-fitting shoes, adjusts a hard pillow, and slowly stretches out her weary body. Through her "window" she can still glimpse the nervous one across the street. She admires the clothes and the recently cut hair and imagines how those excellent shoes must feel. She smiles without happiness, wondering the source of all the anxious hurry.

1

Many of us in the American middle class are spiritually homeless. We have better roofs than the genuinely poor but not better foundations. Rich in things, Fosdick said, but poor in soul.

We are as underdeveloped spiritually as any majority-world nation—as immature in our spiritual infrastructure as some of them are with regard to technology. Likewise, "three-quarters" nations have inner wealth that we can only barely understand.

The jokes in Hungary, I learned while there, are infinitely better than our own and told with much greater verve and frequency. An African-American friend of mine told me that "poor people have to know God. What else do they have?" I wish I could say that I heard without envy either the jokes or the word about the poor and God. I did not. I have been well trained to want everything.

These awful polarities between inner wealth and outer poverty, outer wealth and inner poverty, probably also exist between the two women on the street. The woman who lives in the cardboard box surely knows more about her own inner strength than the one who is becoming anxious over a missed taxicab. What I covet is good shoes for the woman who lives in a box and inner strength for the woman whose shoes have never pinched—both/and, not either/or. While I could never imagine placing one of the polarities over the other—because both are clearly essential to what we know of human life—still there are those who will judge my own envy. Wanting inner wealth while having so much (relative) outer wealth is clearly some sort of crime, one that comes directly from the inner poverty itself.

Like many in the First World, I imagine, sinfully, that the poor have great sex, great jokes, great "spirituality." I am "disciplined"; they are not. My discipline gave me money; their lack of discipline gives them great sex. The errors are abundant in confessing the lust for inner wealth that I share with the lady in the fine shoes. Let me confess them all here: the racism, the envy, the projection. Let me also say that I know the larger part of the sin. It is the way my own inner poverty, my own spiritual homelessness, causes cardboard boxes to spring up all over town. Because I am not rich enough to care, other women's feet pinch—if they have shoes—all over the world. There is a connection between my wealth and their poverty: it is the spiritual indifference that results from living a spiritually homeless life.

Dare I say that I imagine homing and housing myself spiritually might result in better homes for everyone? No, that is not all it will take. But it is not a bad place for me to start. And it is the only place that I really can start. Missing this step of making myself a home—becoming a being who is at home—would kill even the best government program or renaissance of American business. It may already have: both the War on Poverty and the riches of the 1980s failed to make a difference in the lives of people on the street. If anything, there are more people in substandard housing today proportionately than at any other time in American history. Why?

I don't really know. Nor do the genuine experts on the matter. But I do know that I join many Americans in inhabiting a caring deficit, a compassion fatigue, a selfishness that makes me oddly capable of stepping over homeless people on the way to my cab. Were I less capable of not caring, and more capable of caring, surely solutions to actual homelessness would be more possible. More politically possible. More spiritually possible. More materially possible. Well-sheltered people can care. Spiritually homeless people cannot.

Making myself a home is not just for me. But first it is for me. Practically and actually, it is for me.

The great American writer James Thurber made his career out of exaggerating American anxiety. He wrote about a cousin who fears going to sleep because he might stop breathing, and about a grandmother who lives afraid that the electricity might spill out of the wires. Their fear is totally out of proportion to their essential security, but they don't know it. Not knowing their security is their problem. What Thurber showed lovingly and humorously is that the inner is the site of great weakness for the American. We love his window on our fears because he was able—most of the time—to also love our fears.

One of the great Thurber images is that of a bird in a cage stuck in Sing Sing. The little joke about song contained in the starker imprisonment gives us a couple of hints about how to apprehend our larger American polarity. We are doubly trapped: as rich people in inner poverty and as poor people in outward poverty. I think of the bird because it also suggests the heart of the heart of the matter. Something deep inside is what is really stuck. I like to think of that bird getting out, all the way out, and singing us around Sing Sing. When I speak of shelter for the spiritually homeless, I have an image of a caged bird singing: coming out—getting beyond the layers of fear that barricade the doors of our hearts; getting those two women to cross the street that separates them and their imprisoned, interconnected worlds.

Here I want to argue the both/and of inner and outer wealth, inner and outer shelter, as the human possibility we may all dare covet for each other. I think of a child I met on the Croatian border. She was clinging to a stale piece of bread, and would not remove her hand from the pocket that held the bread. Finally a relief worker was located who spoke her particular dialect. Or so we think. It might be instead that just enough time had passed.

The child let the relief worker know that the piece of bread was given to her by her mother. It was the last time the child saw the mother before she disappeared. The bread made her think her mother might come back. There was little chance that her mother might ever return. That child's hand on her bread is something I will never forget.

At the same time, I was worried about my own children. As card-carrying, white, middle-class kids, they resent their mother's international travel. Or even her daily trip to the office. They think she should be "there" (which means with them). They covet any time she spends with the kind of woman who lives in cardboard boxes or children who clutch stale bread. More is their middle name; less the name of the majority of children around the world. There is no reason I should "bean" them with this information now. They will have to find out themselves. The clash between spiritual homelessness and actual refugees is one that does not leave my own door or heart or passport. To me it seems the most real fact in the world. I have so much; so many have so little. This fact is basic.

One night we were sitting in our backyard enjoying a barbecue. Just as fork lifted to mouth, a loud thud was heard in the road in the front. It is a bad road; many car accidents happen there. We knew what had happened. But we didn't know how parabolic it was. A new white van had been hit by an old black car. The old black car turned out to be driven by an uninsured, unlicensed Hispanic man. The white car turned out to be driven by an insured, licensed white man. Within seconds after impact, the white man, as I observed directly, ran across to the Hispanic man, screaming, "Who is going to pay for the damages?" A six-months-pregnant woman holding a one-year-old screaming child was coming out of the passenger seat. The white man did not inquire about her state, nor that of the child's. "Who," said he, "is going to pay for the damages?"

The police arrived. They immediately arrested the unlicensed man, unceremoniously, hands up against the cruiser. I don't know whether they checked the license of the white man. I can't find out, because the police are angry with me for questioning the proceedings that night. The woman and child were left with me on the side of the road. I took them to the police station later.

The child's pacifier had been left in the black car. While we were sitting there waiting to see what would happen to its driver, the child was screaming loudly. I went to the drugstore to buy a pacifier for "Julia." The store was closed. But I saw a young woman who had also been disappointed by the store's being closed. I asked her if she was going to the local grocery store to make her purchase. Yes, she said. I thrust three dollars into her hand and asked if she would get a pacifier and bring it to the police station. I explained the reason. With an all-American, nearly Cover Girl confidence and humor, she said, "Aye, aye, captain." It was then that I knew to whom this book should be dedicated. The Cover Girl. She wanted to help. She wanted to connect. She didn't mind extending her own home, minimal as it probably was if she is an average American college student. If anything, she was waiting to extend it. To fling wide the doors of her tent and to let this little girl in, for a brief significant moment. She wanted to be invited to a spiritual home.

She came to the police station a few minutes later, thrust the pacifier and the crumpled three dollars in my hand, and rushed off.

History has this shape to me. An unlicensed, uninsured, uncollateralized black car has veered off the road and hit our van. The road is bad. Our middle-class question is, "Who is going to pay for the damages?" My answer in this book is that *we* are going to pay for the damages. When we become spiritually well enough to want to—to not want to live another moment without trying to.

We are not well enough yet to want to: we will be.

The physically homeless woman is condemned to useless being. The spiritually homeless woman is condemned to useless doing. Both need what the other has. When we are spiritually homed, we will find ourselves more available to physical homing. It won't seem the mountain of difficulty it now looks like. The price won't be so high because we will begin to assess damages differently. Our soul will be as important to us as our vans, and we will care what happens to both. Likewise, we will care what happens to the old cars as well as the old, well-used souls. We will find out that in the beginning God put soul and body together, married them as the meaning of what it was to be a human. What God has put together, let no one dare tear apart.

WHENCE HOMELESSNESS

It is hard to say when we lost our apartment. Like the genuinely homeless, we have wandered for a long time. Was it vocational zest about our job that we first lost? Or was it our family whom we haven't seen for more than a year? Or the failures of our marriages to look like the movies said they would? Or just the recession that made us too scared to tell our boss to stop pinching our behinds? Or was it some larger and longer personal devaluation? Or something bigger, or some combination of bigger things, such as capitalism and secularism and industrialism, the loss of the family farm, the leeching of the ozone, the topsoil erosion?

Whence homelessness of the spiritual kind? It is to begin to think that you have no control over your home,...that "we" have no power over "them."

Unfortunately, all these things are a stream leading to the river of spiritual homelessness. They join our own scandal in letting them happen. These outsiders found willing colonies in us. We didn't even fight that much.

I am a partisan of localism. I believe we lost our homes when things got too big. As schools consolidated and experts told us we didn't know how to educate our own children. As cars encouraged us to move farther out, to not be happy nearby. As state and national government took over bureaucratic control of life, from cradle to grave. As the possibility of kindergarten became the necessity of kindergarten, and children left home earlier and earlier, both in life and to catch the bus in the morning. As the two-career family became the latest answer to the latest populism, convincing feminists that we really didn't do anything valuable in caring for children and drinking coffee with each other. As "down" time became a sin and being "on" a virtue. As the Protestant work ethic went from ethic to obligation. As the number of Julias in the world went from many to millions.

I am neither right nor left in my diagnosis. I was formed in that part of the sixties that disdained "liberals" and, though I have voted Democratic for some time now, I really don't like big solutions to human problems. They don't work. Small solutions do work. Parables were Jesus' weapon in the world; parabolic shelter is also mine. Because I have had the grace to know plenty of people who keep themselves at home in an increasingly ridiculous society, I believe in their local solutions to complex problems. I even practice local solutions to larger problems myself. Sometimes I am successful; mostly I row upstream.

When I began to think of this book, my husband put the question to me hard. Have you ever really known spiritual shelter? No, I had to admit. But I have lived in some mighty fine hotels. I've pitched some gorgeous tents.

Whence homelessness? The inner acquiescence to outer greed. The being a part of something that hurts us. Systemic problems internalized and agreed to. Standing around and letting things get big. Letting the small grocery stores move out of the center of town so everybody *had* to have a car rather than a neighbor close by.

We may not be able to rearrange all the parts of either our big or our small worlds. But we can pitch tents. We can take rooms in the better hotels, the ones that shelter us and don't rob us of our self-respect. We don't have to live the way capitalism, secularism, industrialism, or post-industrialism orders us to. We can live our own way, even if we have to live their way "part-time." Our full-time job is sheltering ourselves and our families. We may have to live on the edge of this society to do that, but there, with each other, we can pitch a tent.

I know a lot of people who have pitched tents. One of my friends is a lawyer and her husband is a contractor. They take care of their own children by splitting their shift. She was previously in a committed lesbian relationship. He had the joy one day of telling a coworker, who was complaining about "dykes," to shut up, that his wife was a lesbian. When she ran for town office, her platform stressed local solutions to local problems. She wanted the town to start recycling the waste that came into it, at the least, and to reduce the waste stream at best. People thought she was crazy: why bother protecting our land? "They" are going to ruin it anyway.

Whence homelessness of the spiritual kind? It is to begin to think that you have no control over your home, or the land on which it sits. It is to believe that democracy is a joke, that "we" have no power over "them," the ones who are ruining our life.

Other friends still run a family farm. They lose money right and left. Their children think they are crazy, but they like what they are doing, and believe in it. An actor friend of ours works when he can; he has been broke for a long time. But he knows Shakespeare perhaps better than most living Americans. Status and salary, no; shelter, yes. There are differences. Status, salary, and shelter are so regularly confused among Americans that it is only the rare among us who can tell the difference. Far too many left their love, whether farm or stage, to work for "security." I know very few for whom the bargain worked. Instead, by killing their spirits, they have also killed their security. They live without a home in their best self. And that commute from best self to compromised self, that lack of residence, has polluted our land and polluted our spirits. We are ashamed of what we have done to the land as well as to the old women living in cardboard boxes. Shame has become the home of many Americans.

Whence homelessness? It comes after the shame of letting democracy squeeze right out of our hands.

Moving away from the house of shame is very difficult. Genuine security, meaningful jobs, working for a real person instead of a giant corporation each are rare in our world today. Salary and status still call our name, even when we have regular work. If they don't call yours, they surely do call mine. Sometimes they even convince me that they are shelter, and sometimes they are. You have to live without a paycheck for only a short time to know how nice it is when one shows up. Many Americans also find there is a lot of week left at the end of the money. Most of us in the middle class do receive the status of salary with a regular check. But we also wait in fear for the other shoe to drop. What do I have to pay the paycheck for paying me? Too often it's not just labor we exchange for our checks: it is also dignity and freedom.

Whence homelessness? It is the mistaken substitution of security for shelter.

The evidence for spiritual homelessness is in the way so many can still be so sad, even with regular paychecks and regular work. And the evidence for spiritual home is the way so many also find their way out of the house of shame into genuine security. We two-time our life if our work is not a home. It is no accident that leisure is as important to Americans as it is.

You may have other answers for the gone-wrongness and the consequent lack of shelter. Bigness is my diagnosis; smallness my cure. Little tents, parabolic solutions, gestures that show us and the world that we haven't given up on owning our own actual land and democratic land.

Bigness is surely reason for our lost apartment. False security replaced genuine security. We bought other people's solutions and salvation for our lives. We were conquered by packaging, by cardboard boxes instead of firm foundations. And we live in shame about how low our price was.

The evidence that we can find our way out is that so many do. The rare American lives a fully spiritually sheltered life all the time, but the American who is on a journey to more serious shelter is common. He or she searches through leisure, self-help books, religious faith, politics, acting, gardening—through a million efforts to find a way home. Joining those efforts is the purpose of this book. I think of our search as a form of partnership with Julia's mother. We are searching for the same thing; we just approach it from opposite sides of the table.

She is going to want a world where an ambulance might think her fetus is important enough to be sent for. In a similar situation, mine surely would have enjoyed that overprotection that night. I am wanting a world where someone will send an ambulance for my soul so I don't have to be worried about its apparent shriveling.

BUILDING BLOCKS

One child asked the child psychiatrist Bruno Bettelheim, as the doctor gave him some blocks, whether he was about to play a "fun" game or a "winning" game. Bettelheim assured him that playing with blocks was a fun game. There was no "right" way to do it. Spiritual shelter is more a fun game than a winning game: the fun is along the way as much as when you get there. Just acknowledging the journey, just throwing the colonists out, is a step out of the Sing Sing of shame—or at least out of the birdcage.

Another famous psychologist, Carl Jung, said that we all smuggle our personal psychology into everything we say and do. That means that my spiritual house will be different from yours and that that is good. If they were all the same, as they are in the spiritually homeless world, where security is disguised as uniformity, that would mean that they weren't meant for us to dwell in. Rather, they were meant for General Humans to dwell in. We are not General Humans, there should not be General Foods, and there should not be General Motors. Spiritual shelter is something particular and

Many of us are building in a ritualized way when we clean our houses.... Shelter is the ordering of chaos.

something different for everyone: some even build houses that the current economy would like! That bugs people like me, who don't like the current economic arrangements, but that's fine. I value diversity more than uniformity; choice more than compulsion. I want to live with people who are at home. It is safer and more interesting. As long as I can also have similar choices and live the way I want to as "particular human," I don't care if others express their particular human in a more generalized way.

That's why I brought up my formerly lesbian friend: she is choosing a different way. She needs to be protected in her choices.

I am long past the snobbery against ranch houses or trailers that the truly utopian enjoy. What matters is the spiritual, economic, and political process around home, not the actual place. What matters is that our spirits direct our economy and our politics. That doesn't happen much in the U.S. today.

For me to begin the fun of building my spiritual shelter, I needed to start with ordinary time. I had to stop breakfast from being invaded by telephone calls from work. I had to keep Sabbath. I had to make sure there was some time that I could call my own and steal it back from the thousand bosses who thought it was theirs. That included the PTA as well as my paying boss, my husband, my mother, and all three of my children. And I had to remember to take a walk and touch the soil in my garden daily. That play—and getting my work time released for that play— became a heroic quest. I realized no one wanted me to play: they wanted me to work. After seeing how much I was a person living in a spiritual cardboard box, I had to get hold of my time. I considered it a major accomplishment that I sat down on my rug and picked up a block.

Carl Jung describes a memory from his tenth or eleventh year—when he had been a passionate builder of blocks—that he used to create a rite for himself. "I began accumulating suitable stones, gathering them and building:

cottages, a castle, a whole village. I went on with my building game after the noon meal every day....Naturally, I
thought about the significance of what I was doing, and
asked myself, now, really, what are you about? You are
building a small town, and doing it as if it were a rite!"
(*Memories, Dreams, Reflections* by C.G. Jung, edited by Amelia
Jaffe, Pantheon Books, 1963.)

Those of us who are spiritually homeless need to do
what Jung did. We need to return as a kneeling child to our
rug and there build—and build sacramentally.

We probably already know how. Many of us are building in a ritualized way when we clean our houses. We are
creating a home. We are giving ourselves the gift of shelter.
Shelter is the ordering of chaos. The genuinely homeless
woman arranged her cardboards once she got in them.
Shelter is also the place we go to get out of the rain, the
place of less exposure to the elements. If we can think of
the satisfaction of making our place "clean," of making it
just the way we like it, we can begin the ritualized gathering
of the spiritual blocks and stones that will take us back
home. We will be led by that pleasure to a place of less risk
and exposure.

Very few middle-class people in this culture think there
is an unexposed place: we are on duty twenty-four hours a
day. We all know "this can't last" and that we are building
the wrong kind of world. The sensation of shelter is one we
experience as little as we experience good housekeeping.
There is a connection between the way people used to take
care of their houses and now don't, and the spiritual
homelessness of so many. More people would tell you that
their "house is a mess" than would say otherwise. The
revelation that Gloria Steinem didn't know for years that
her oven didn't work is a great symbol for these end-of-the-
century decades.

We add a block to our foundation by believing that
shelter is something you're allowed and supposed to have.
Religion should guarantee it but does not. Even many of us

raised religiously in this culture ceased to develop spiritually at adolescence. We remain trapped there: our religion wears blue jeans, our spirits are youthfully defiant. What the psychologists call a reaction formation has set in with regard to matters spiritual: all we know is what we don't want—old ways—and whom we don't want to be like—our parents. We have no positive spiritual clarity, just an unfinished set of rebellions. Shelter is less a goal for youth than adventure. When people mature religiously and otherwise, we begin to want different things. We build our way home by growing up religiously; we realize that shelter is not something we *want* but also something we *may* have.

This sense of permission about taking care of our own homes is a major piece of the foundation for our shelter.

Our homeless culture has silenced religion, for the most part, in its declaration that there is more to life than us. More to life than bread or salary or status. We lost the visibility of the heavens from the earth. We believed that our doing was what was supposed to be. We denied ourselves a channel of grace. When we can't do, or don't want to do, we become useless. The failure of doing to sustain us is our spiritual homelessness. Birds caged by doing can't sing. Shelter comes when being grounds doing and makes it graceful.

The strategic trick of finding shelter lies in understanding the size of these obstacles, and using a fun game to get through them. Grace is very much the equal of the obstacles but we have to access it. Accessing grace in our day means revolution. Decolonization. It means denying our denial and confessing that we in fact played no small part in letting our country become what it is. We are not victims of capitalism or any of the big "isms." We let their consequences happen to us. We can un-let. As large as the obstacles are, still larger is the grace of the small person who is in touch with a large God. God did not intend the way things are. God's intentions are mansions. Shelters. Many rooms. A place prepared for us, parabolically, in small ways, small gestures, small directions. The strategy of grace is to show just how large the small really is.

As we reach for our spiritual homes, we get their strength. Ray Bradbury said that first you jump, then you get your wings. We allow ourselves to be as we do. I needed to walk and think and meditate for as long as I needed to march. There is no need to stop marching, not for me or my genuinely homeless counterpart. She has responsibilities for justice just as I do. We need to bring our blocks, our picnics, our children, our music, our cards—and sit in public places with homeless people. Signs of life. Signs of shelter. Sappho said, "Find Peace—and others will follow you anywhere."

Mature spirituality, with its grand and awkward connections to history and others and to self, appears to many like a mess of Legos on a child's rug—and each piece seems too difficult for small hands to manipulate. But a house is made by a series of connections. We will find spiritual shelter when we find a friend, a connection, a relationship where both our shelter and homelessness are allowed to be. We will find shelter as soon as we stop ordering building plans and begin to build our own way, with our own blocks.

An Outline of This Book

After we have given ourselves permission to build, and to build our way, and after we have given ourselves permission to have fun while building, we look around. We see what people have used for centuries to make themselves a spiritual home. Here we will look at the way failure is actually a building block for a spiritual home. We start usually in a bit of rubble, in the awareness of not being at home despite outward appearances. Then we will look at new ways of seeing: how do we find the largeness of the small? Parabolic thinking is one answer to that question. Then we will look at inner resources, how the key to our spiritual house is already in our pocket. We simply have to realize its presence. Then we will look at the paradox of shelter, that its very spiritual presence in our lives will make us quickly more available to adventure, to journey, to going out rather than just going in. Then we will look at practical stuff, such as jobs and place and money and children. Obligations and how they connect to spiritual shelter. Finally, we will look at spiritual strategy: how do we put a spiritually sheltered life together? The closing chapter is called "Traveling Light." It is less a building block than interior decoration, the final stage of being at home in our own spirits.

FAILURE IS A BUILDING BLOCK

The biggest actor in my life during the last decade has been the recession that first dehumanized the poor and now is eating away at the middle class. During the time of this leading man on my stage, I have also been trying to build a spiritual shelter for myself. On the political level and pastoral level and communal level I have been a ridiculous failure. I am fighting for things my partners and I had won twenty years ago. Things such as the right to choose an abortion, decent working conditions and hours, humane health care, funded education—all are hanging on by a string. Some say there is insufficient money for these things. Others know that there is plenty of money, that many Americans don't want to spend the money on peace or justice. We pay for protection, not peace or justice. Locally, more cops; nationally, excessive defense. To build a spiritual home while living the life of a political failure is the challenge.

Olive Schreiner, a great feminist in a nonfeminist moment, quotes Elizabeth Barrett Browning to describe the way she

We must get beyond the loss of upward mobility as the controlling metaphor for our lives and into something that makes more decent and human sense.

21

also misfit her time: "What I aspired to be and was not comforts me." To learn the trick of quiet in the middle of change—and to dedicate my calm to the tension of my times—that describes the shelter I'm after. I have it only some of the time; that I aspire for it, despite its fluctuating presence, comforts me.

If I had not known these failures, if life had continued to be what was promised me as a child, I might never have even started to look for spiritual shelter. My satisfaction would have gotten in the way. As it is, some of my home burned down. I am building in rubble. Most of us do.

Invaders, like history or recession or plain bad luck, are the rubble in which we either build or fail to build. Seeing shelter as only personal, interior, or religious is a lopped-off way of being spiritual. Outer events give us the gift of enough failure to begin to go inside and see if anyone is home. Daily shelter is a combination of inner and outer events integrated in that doing/being we know as person. A personal shelter will do nothing for a political failure—because it is the failure of the polis that causes much of the homelessness in the first place. The very mythology of individual change or protection has to be repositioned in ordinary life: it is keeping us from shelter much more than history is.

I'm not building shelter just for me.

Failure is a building block to shelter. My son's first grade teacher saw how easily he was taking to reading. She told us at his first conference that she was going to give him a much harder book, one that he couldn't quite manage. Why? So his first experience with difficulty and failure was not at too late a point in his life for him to adapt to it. This recession came too late in most baby boomers' lives for us to adapt to it. The spiritual theme for many right now is grieving and loss: how do we let go of all that we thought we had but have no more? How do we look our downward mobility straight in the eye and learn to be its friend?

"Think not to settle down for ever in any truth, but use it as a tent in which to pass a summer night, but build no house of it, or it will become your tomb" (Earl Balfour, from *A Tent in Which to Pass a Summer's Night* by Belle Valerie Gaunt and George Trevelyan, Coventure, London, 1977).

The child knocks down as much as he or she builds up. The block metaphor has applied so much to my life that I have come to love its companionship. I wanted life to be so simple, I wanted to make my midlife adjustment to simplicity and sufficiency, to raise my young children in something I imagined as normal. Instead, I was handed more tragedy and more complexity than I had ever imagined. The recession literally turned the main street of my community into a ghost town. My church was on Main Street. The best way for me to really cheat my children was to refuse to acknowledge the reality of this recession and the burden it genuinely is to so many, the way they were raised directly in its historical shadow.

One third of my congregation was unemployed at this time; dozens of people came daily through the door looking for food and lost self-respect. Once I was held hostage by a drug-crazed ex-Marine. Three times blood spilled in fights on the floor of our church's soup kitchen. Disconnecting from this reality could be my tomb: connecting to it will give me shelter.

A wise man said that what it really means to be a contemplative is to stay connected to what is real—that anything else is a scared caricature. I think of myself as an urban, station-wagon-driving monk. I want to stay connected to this strange reality of loss that has turned up to civilize and sacralize, rather than facilitate, my days. I stay connected by revising my shelter daily—like a child would rebuild the building she built yesterday, adding and resolving new conflicts or waiting for inspiration for the next one.

We need a new theme for our days. Upward mobility was the theme we were raised in. That theme is gone. How about the theme of sustainability? (What if we get bored?)

The theme of justice? (What if there really isn't enough to go around?) The theme of participation? (What if some people really like to be told what to do?) The theme of leisure? (What if technology really doesn't work to release us from work?) These are the kinds of questions that adults need to sit on their rugs and mull over and experiment with, block after block, day after day. We must get beyond the loss of upward mobility as the controlling metaphor for our lives and into something that makes more decent and human sense.

We will hardly be the first generation to have to re-learn their lives. The great myth of Zarathrustra is a good way to understand how stages impact daily living. In Zarathrustra there are three stages to the life of the spirit. Each involves a return to the life of the child, just as Jesus advised that we must become as little children to enter the kingdom of heaven and just as Isaac found that he had to keep going back to the beginning, back to the original well. Freud and Jung weighed in fairly heavily on this notion of return as well, saying that adult builders need to revisit childhood to go on.

In the teachings of Zarathrustra, the first stage of the spirit is that of the camel. The camel gets down on his knees and says, "Put a load on me." This is the condition of youth and learning. When the camel is well loaded, he rises to his feet and runs out into the desert. This is the place where he's going to be alone to find himself and then be transformed into a lion. The function and deed of the lion is to kill a dragon. On every scale of the dragon, a law is written, some dating from 2000 B.C., others from yesterday's paper. When the dragon is killed, the lion is transformed into a child. The child returns to the spontaneity and innocence and thoughtlessness of rules so marvelous in childhood. I covet such a stage for our culture as well as for me as an individual.

The Buddhists, in a famous woodcut, tell the story of the twelve stops on the journey of the man and the ox. First he must find the ox, then he must learn to ride it; then he walks it, loses it, finds it again, abandons it; then he has to walk alone, reachieve his original harmony with it, and return home to the village from whence he started. Again our culture by means of its redundancies is begging us to mount such oxen and to learn how to ride them home. Our religious experience is still so uninformed and immature that we are not even aware of the journey, much less its possible conclusions.

All the world religions tell us that we must change in order to stay in relationship with our spiritual home. Exile and return must mark our days, "our coming in and our going out," as the Hebrew Bible puts it.

These ancient stories remind us of the great circles of the spirit. It is the child who wants to return home but also wants to grow up. Such staging and development are clearly part of the paradox of shelter. The child returns to the posture of learning. I had to learn all over at age forty that my productive capacity—all that I could do for others— couldn't save me. Or them. Or anything. If anything, at the corner I needed to turn, doing more would probably kill me. I had to learn how to do less and still be me. I had to learn how to live in real history, not the mythological one promised by my past. I had to develop what Paul Ricoeur calls the second naïveté, the return to childhood simplicity as a failed and complicated adult.

It was as though I was confronted with the building blocks, Legos, Lincoln Logs, Tinker Toys, and told to come up with a new home, one that required all your internal individual stuff but was released from the anxious individuality of it all. I had no idea what it even looked like. Nor does any child who sits on a rug and picks up blocks. We make anew. We make without maps. We find shelter written on the back of our brains or the bottom of the cave of our stomach, unless we get stuck in an old stage, near a dried-up well, and don't have the courage to change. We may think we are making a choice to keep ourselves sheltered—

as in that ridiculously revered roof over our heads—but we are actually choosing spiritual homelessness.

For our days to be homes in which we can live, we must journey with the oxen and follow the path of the ones who know something about the inner life. It doesn't matter if Jesus' story or Moses' story or Mohammed's story makes the most sense to you. Each guarantees a home and guarantees that it is there in normal days. The challenge of spiritual homelessness is its redundancy: the very experience of its pain is a beckoning to travel more deeply. Not to travel more deeply somewhere else, but to travel more deeply right where we are—and to find the stage of our days so that they may shelter us. The rubble releases many gifts. It lets us dig.

PARABLES ABOUT SHELTER

Shelter for the spiritually homeless comes in the shape of parables, little stories, small moments, timeless times, being in a place while you are in the place. Like Jesus' stories about corn that gets picked on the Sabbath, or water that develops into wine, or grapes that workers pick, or seed that farmers sew, shelter is something common, not grand. It is temporary, not permanent. It is an awareness of the meaning in a moment.

In *Postcards from the Edge*, a movie that came out in the eighties, a woman writes a card to her friend, "Having great time. Wish I was here." Shelter is the opposite of her sentiment. It is having a good time, glad I am here.

Parables let me reach for the utopia, the "what should be." They take regular reality and transform it.

That's why I talk of shelter as parabolic. As wresting the meaning from the moment, seeing it without overseeing or overstating it. It is the grand room in the hotel or the tent on the edge of spiritual town. A place from which we see the meaning in our moments.

A good example of what I mean is contained in the modern phrase "quality time." It is what we substituted for parenting when everybody went to work. Quality time with children has at least two unrelated features. One is that you manage to stand by while they are having fun. Like when they finally get a triple skip out of a skinny beach stone and you manage to look up from your chair at the beach to watch that stone skip its trinity, just at the right time. Quality time also involves being there at the moment the knee is scraped and the child still thinks he or she is bleeding to death. The rest of the time you're not really needed. Quality time is showing up—in Woody Allen's great phrase about what matters in life. It is being there when you are there. It is not a mad dash home for fifteen minutes of an unwanted card game. Similarly, shelter is not grand planned gestures but being there when things happen, both to ourselves and to those we love.

There is a double bind in this matter of quality time with children: you are always needed. You just don't know when. For the spiritually homeless, drifting to find shelter may take a lot of waiting around. That, too, is time at home.

We have unusual relationships with time in the modern world. There are few of us who think we're not too busy. And so we rush through all sorts of life, thinking we are on the way to somewhere else. If home, then work; if work, then home. We are on the way so much that we forget that part of home is the way.

I live with a lot of guilt for taking shortcuts. Some nights my children don't get pajamas; I often put them to bed directly in their clothes. I do my correspondence in other people's meetings. Sometimes I even double-time my own. I always brush my wet hair in the car. I have even given sermons with wet hair.

If you think that shortcuts are only superficial in my overdone life, you are wrong. I miss deep moments. I fake hard decisions. I also neglect the important.

But I also have plentiful moments of grace. Some of my best laughs are in my car. I realize that this morning's breakfast at home was shelter: we spoke, touched, connected.

We didn't overstate the connection as I might do on a day "off." We let it happen while we were "on."

Another busy friend of mine raises golden retrievers. She had to get to her daughter's Little League game, and the time had come for the puppies to be delivered. She put the mother dog in the van, and watched the game from the front seat. In the back seat five babies were born.

I call her a real efficiency expert—somebody who had a lot to do and did it. I have moved from guilt to grace about double-timing by the parable of her grace under pressure. She helped me have another image of the short-cut. I have discovered a way to be kind to the shortcutting self. It is the grace in the grind, not the grace above the grind. I'll have time for that grace later. Now I need to double-time.

Even reaching for this kind of grace is gracious. Is shelter. Is time when we are protected by the shed of a larger grace that keeps us from the gruesome elements of our own lives. The very reach for grace in the grind is a gracious act. I have found that even an extreme double-timer like me has a good reach. The very reason I double-time and triple-time and work the edges—and also affront the margins and the Sabbath and large parts of the Holy—is out of respect for the grind. I love puppies. And pajamas. And giving sermons. And wet hair. I am so urgent for life, not just one, but two or three, that I can't imagine not reaching for them all. I was born with low blood pressure, so that helps. And I don't mind making mistakes. I used to be humiliated by them; now I expect them. Going this fast requires them. Things get lost on the short routes and on the shortcuts.

But even in the short routes and the shortcuts, there is shelter. There are arms around us that are not our own.

I have a recurring dream. In the first segment I am attached by large chains to all my projects, which are nicely penned on 3" x 5" cards. Volunteer at the soup kitchen. Call Aunt Sue. Pick up saxophone. Return wrong saxophone.

Pick up music book for saxophone. Return wrong music book for right music book. Repair all time-saving appliances. Brush teeth. Effect world peace. Write congressperson. Update dryer maintenance agreement. Change batteries in smoke alarms. Read great books. Kiss the children. Give each one a belly button. Find missing husband.

In the bad part of the dream, just to walk, I have to literally move each chain all by itself. When the chains come, I know it is time to go sit in the back of the van with the hypothetical puppies. I am tired. Grind has outwitted grace. I need to be reborn.

Then I rest. Soon the dream will return, but this time each project will be attached to my same less-drooped shoulders by crocheted lace. I am not even walking on the ground in the next dream so light are my steps, so airy the attachment of me to my projects. I have found the grace in the grind. Or, better, the grace in the grind has found me. I am no longer trudging.

I am sheltered rather than homeless. I have a spiritual home, a place to rest. The place is the pillow in the grind, not the pillow above the grind.

This grace under the grind has shown me the virtue in what some call workaholism and I call a love of work. Not always. But often enough to keep me confident of the return of grace. I can even go a while on empty. I know grace will return sooner if I rest, but sometimes I am too tired to rest. Grace in the grind is more loving to me than grace separated could ever be. It is like the joy of coming back from a trip: the old house looks even better than we remembered.

For me, the self-discovery is the more grind, the more grace. Chains turn to lace.

Can we be at home in the grind? I hope so. There aren't many places where the grind is far. Shelter for the spiritually homeless is not winning the lottery and spending the rest of our life in the Bahamas. It is shelter in, not above, the grind.

Another parable. All the boys in the eighth grade came to school with shaved heads. The reason? One boy had chemotherapy and all his hair had fallen out. They shaved in solidarity with him, so "he wouldn't feel funny." Can we be sheltered even with cancer? Of course. Our home is radiation-proof, in a sense. Our home has to do with whom we can touch and who can touch us. Connection to each other is shelter also.

My friend Valerie says it is time to look at the whole world from the point of view of Ezekiel's sneakers. She's right. What she means is that we will see more of what really holds us and holds the world if we look at the world from the bottom up, from the point of view of the kids who feel even more homeless than we do. It is easy to find a home if all you see is the unfolded laundry and the dishwasher and the boss's plans for your day. Or at least easier. But to begin to see home as challenged by cancer in kids or despairing sneakers is to begin to really see. To get through the clutter to the important. Parabolic eyes pick up the clutter so the main frame can be seen. The main frame of reality includes the suffering and the clutter—when we really see, when parables open our eyes and let us see, we also see the arms around the world. They are God's arms and they hold you and me, and Ezekiel and his sneakers.

"A map of the World that does not include Utopia is not worth even glancing at, for it leaves out the one country at which Humanity is always landing." So said Oscar Wilde. For me, part of shelter is the picture of what might be. The children all with shaved heads or Ezekiel's sneakers as joyful as opposed to despairing. Or my laundry folded before midnight. Parables let me reach for the utopia, the "what should be." They take regular reality and transform it.

One of the great crises in my life occurred when people began to trash my favorite utopia, the sixties, the time when I came of age. They put out a word that said they weren't really home when I knew in my heart that they had been. Joan Nestle said, "The sixties are the favorite target of people who take delight in the failure of dreams." I have had to find shelter in remembering my dreams, in continuing to posit a utopia, and in the failure of dreams. Both are possible. Both views need parables to carry them. Little stories that mean a lot.

Edwin Friedman finds shelter in a different place than the spot between dream or fulfillment, or in dream, or failure of dream. He also finds shelter in the found. "What we find is much better than what we set out to find. The found is better than the sought. Even Magellan and Columbus and Verrazano knew that." When we say that little stories show us our shelter, what we mean is that we are alert on the way. We are looking for the meaning, actively. The meaning may be in the dream. Or in the failure of the dream. Or in the replacement of the dream, in the found. The shelter is in the alertness. The shelter allows us to live beyond the meaning we thought we were supposed to have into the meaning that we do have.

Sheltering ourselves by alertness to parables—by parabling our lives—means living beyond our resentments and angers, even if they are totally just. The Dalai Lama shows no anger toward the Chinese, even though the policy of the Chinese government for years has been to practice genocide toward Tibetans. When asked about his apparent lack of anger, by an incredulous reporter at the time he won the Nobel Peace Prize, the Dalai Lama replied something to the effect that, "They have taken everything from us; should I let them take my mind as well?"

Shelter is so solid in its sense that the arms of God are around us and the world that we are at home even in anger and resentment. We still own ourselves. No one steals us.

In the Kabir, a sacred text, a poet long ago warned,

Don't go outside your house to see the flowers.
My friend, don't bother with that excursion.
Inside your body there are flowers.
One flower has a thousand petals.

That will do for a place to last.
Sitting there you will have a glimpse of beauty
Inside the body and out of it,
Before gardens and after gardens.

Does this advice mean that we cannot be angry or disappointed? Of course not. Anger or disappointment doesn't make us homeless. They are part of the home. I sent my friend who lost her garden the poem about inner flowers. She may hate it. Her garden is gone. She lives on the third floor now. But at least I put my inadequate arms around her loss. It was an attempt at shelter.

When Gandhi was assassinated at pointblank range, he put his palms together in his prayerful way toward his attacker, uttered his mantra, and died. He was able to bring the lifelong discipline of nonattachment to his dying. He had known his life was in constant danger. He embodied his own vision of political and spiritual freedom. His personal well-being was of limited value in comparison. He was always putting it on the line. He died at home and lived at home.

The Master sees things as they are,
Without trying to control them.
She lets them go their own way.
And resides at the center of the circle.
            —*Lao-Tzu, Tao-Te-Chung*

The spiritual masters see shelter as something that includes the uninvited guests of anger and resentment. So may we if we use their life and their work as parabolic for our own.

John Donne reminds us of our connection one with another, the permission we have to use poetry and people as parables:
No Man is an Island
Entire of itself

Every man is a piece of the continent, a part of
    the main
If a clod be washed away by the sea
Europe is the less, as well as if a promontory were
As well as if a manor of thy own friends or thine
    own were
Any man's death diminishes me; because I am
    involved in mankind.
And therefore, never send to know for whom the
    bell tolls.
It tolls for thee.
                              —*John Donne, Meditation XVII*

Parables are not only from the fancy or the famous.
"Regular" people are part of the arms around each one of
us. Driving back at night from Ashland, over the mountain,
beside the stream, house after rural house, I watch all the
lights on the TV screens. It is the little hearth around which
the entire world gathers, when it is not sitting at its day
screen. I am warmed by the way we do the same thing. In
our shelters. In our easy chairs. Shelter may not be just
sitting at home comfortably at night, watching TV, but it is
also that.

Similarly, we don't need electricity or screens or TV to
be at home.

Some nations are overdeveloped physically and underdeveloped spiritually. Other nations are the opposite. Some
people are the same. I think I'd prefer to be the "two-
thirds" world, but maybe that's because I just had dinner.
Shelter for the spiritually homeless is as accessible as shelter
for the physically hungry; they have the same root: A capacity to see that we are held, that there is a roof over our
heads and a foundation under our feet—the heavens and
the earth—even if the place is Calcutta or Ashland.

"What lies behind us and what lies before us are tiny
matters compared to what lies within us." So said Oliver
Wendell Holmes. Within us lies our home.

Our home is the story we stay alert to wherever we are. It is our parable. Every time I hear the song, "I Love to Tell the Story," I hope someone will sing it at my funeral. Telling the story is so much fun. Telling stories is so much fun. It is as good as being home. Or being at church. At "real" church, not at the substitute.

One more parable about how we get to the place called shelter for the spiritually homeless. The day after children's day and Hebrew school were over for the year, nine-year-old Katie announced, "I don't do church in the summer." She needs all her excuses lined out before I object to them. Being an interfaith child in an interfaith family means that she has the pleasure of going to both Sunday school and church and Hebrew school and temple Sunday school—as many as four religious experiences a week. She finds it hard to have that many appointments that, when added to her sports and music and birthday parties, make for an overly full schedule. Even I think her schedule is too full.

So when she announced that she doesn't "do" religion in the summer, I had to stand back and assess my own priorities. Yes, all this religious preparation during the year was important. She wasn't getting out of it. Over the long haul, these lessons will make Katie the educated and faithful person I want her to be—and I'm not even getting to that moment of choice that I know will be hers, eventually. So, no compromise on the religious schooling.

But summers? Should I really invite her to church with me all summer? Or should she go to temple with my husband? Now that the other lessons are over, doesn't she deserve some space?

As I pondered these things, and rushed on with my preparations for church, I realized Katie had gone, unbidden, to the piano. She was enjoying some free time. She was belting out a version of "Joyful, Joyful, We Adore Thee." All on her own. She may not do religion in the summer. But she does praise.

And preparing her to be a person with the priority of praise is what all these lessons are about in the first place. My priority has been fulfilled, and I might have missed it if I had gotten to church on time.

Likewise, I may miss some parables that are the shelter I seek in the first place. I can't even begin to see or hear them all, so many are there. But if I keep my eyes and my ears open, who knows? I may see and hear enough to know that I am not spiritually homeless.

YOUR KEYS ARE IN YOUR POCKET

So much attention is given to those who are physically homeless that we nearly neglect the other scandal, that of spiritual homelessness. Not that one is worse or better than the other! There is no competition between the two. Rather, the growing epidemic of addictions in our land point us straight to the spiritual hunger and the spiritual homelessness of those who don't have enough—or imagine that they don't.

Shelter is having enough where you are. Addiction is the opposite. Addiction is always staying en route to something "more." Addiction is living by the additional; spiritual shelter is the opposite. It is living by what is already with us.

Our mild neurosis is that we don't have enough.... We live as unsheltered people because we think we need something else than what we have.

A while back I got into a frenzy about the location of my car keys. I was late. They were missing. I think most readers have been in such a frenzy, where inadequacy is the name of the moment. Finally, my husband got control of me by saying, "Donna, your keys are in your pocket." For me this remark didn't just save the day. In its deeper message, it saves my life. I have what I need. I don't need to get more.

The same message is healing for those of us who are more than addicts to car trips and "getting things done." We have what we need. Our keys are in our pockets. We don't need a cigarette or a donut or a drink. We don't need to go someplace to improve our life. We can stay where we are. Once this sufficiency of spiritual shelter enters us deeply, we can go places, or maybe even drink fermented beverages. But we don't count on the journey or the beverage to complete us. We are already complete.

Some of what I understand as resurrection is contained in this notion of shelter as adequacy where and as we are. We may not even need our bodies. Eventually even they may go, but our souls will still be saved. And sheltered. What we have in our souls is sufficient. Our keys are in our pockets.

In the small seaside town of Costabel, every morning thousands of starfish are found stranded on the beach. Loren Eisley, the great science writer, tells the story of the starfish in such a way as to throw light on the Easter story. He reports living there for several months and experiencing severe insomnia while there. He would wait for the light and then go out to walk. Every morning he would be joined on the beach by townspeople combing the sand for starfish to kill them for commercial purposes. But one morning, when Eisley got up unusually early, he discovered a solitary man on the beach. He too was gathering starfish but each time he found one alive he would pick it up and throw it as far as he could out beyond the breaking surf, back to the nurturing ocean from which it came. As days went by Eisley found this man embarked on his mission of mercy each morning, seven days a week, no matter the weather.

Eisley named this man "the star thrower," and in a moving meditation he writes of how this man and his predawn work contradicted everything Eisley, the scientist, had been taught about evolution and the survival of the fittest. Here on the beach at Costabel the strong reached down to save, not crush, the weak. Eisley wondered, Is there perhaps a star thrower at work in the universe, a God who contradicts death, a "God whose nature is mercy within mercy within mercy?" (Thomas Merton's words, spoken by Parker Palmer in *Weaving*, March/April 1991, Volume VI, Number 2).

Loren Eisley saw the star thrower as God, as the one who reversed field and gave weakness its chance to live, whereas otherwise the rule of the universe would be that of big fish eating little fish, which just ate smaller ones. We'd always need more to save us when in fact what we need is less. It is a profound image, this solitary figure standing on the beach saving the starfish by throwing them back into the sea from whence they came. It is almost as profound as the image of Easter, that empty tomb, that disappearance of the Christ back to whence he came, in God and heaven, defying death, defying the laws of mortals, and thereby returning the world to its original creation. God intended the world to be Christlike. When the world failed long enough, God sent Jesus, and redeemed the world. Redemption returns us to the clean slate of creation, to the good time before the bad time. Resurrection returns us to where we belong—to our shelter in God—just the way the star thrower returned the starfish to its home. Not without threat. Not without conflict. Not easily. But returned to home, nevertheless.

A more humorous image may show that high fallutin' theories of resurrection are not the only way of saying shelter. Shelter is the simplicity that our keys are in our pocket, that we have what we need. We had an anniversary party recently and our well-linked mild neuroses marched right up, uninvited. He was afraid we didn't have enough food. I was afraid we'd have too much food. He kept going out to the store to buy more food, just in case. I kept hiding the checkbook. Misplacing his wallet. We had, I'd like to report, enough food to feed double the guests we had, assuming they all would have stayed the entire weekend.

Our mild neurosis is that we don't have enough. But we do. We have enough and more, but, like many, we don't know it. We live as unsheltered people because we think we need something else than what we have.

Not just star throwers or party givers or mad house-wives complain about the insufficiency of modern life. I was in Europe recently and many Europeans were complaining about the new common market. One Hungarian told me that the cheese was no longer any good. It had nowhere near its former cream content, before the common market, and thus had begun to taste like American cheese. He wasn't trying to be insulting. Rather, he was recognizing a fact. Before the common market, producers could put any amount of cream they wanted in the Gorgonzola. A double cream Gorgonzola in Paris was as common as a neurotic party giver in Massachusetts. While these Europeans were fussing about the cheese, an African jumped in with his own joke. After ecumenism, he said, according to the lions, all the missionaries tasted the same.

What can all these stories have to do with the way that Jesus emphasizes spiritual food over regular food, spiritual shelter over regular shelter? You have heard it said many times that we don't live by bread alone. That we need a lot less than we think we need. That Jesus' life is a better food than regular food and it is what we need.

Each of the little parables or pictures here is about what matters most to human beings. What matters most to us is our physical life. Our food. What we put on our body. Our raiment.

Our anniversary party was so full of food that we actually had to throw some away. We had more than enough. We have all that we need. But we, both in different ways, don't always know it. We need that gracious visitation from Jesus the Christ to know the peace of heavenly food. Be not afraid, Donna and Warren.

Those lions dare not join the French in complaining about the common market. No matter what silly economists do to regulate the cream content in the cheese, some people will still add a little more. No matter what ecumenists do to turn every church into the same thing, some missionaries will still taste a little juicier. Act a little more flamboyantly. Jazz up the service. No matter how much we fear that the cheese is getting worse, and the church is getting worse, and we are getting worse, we really have no genuine need to fear. We have enough. We have all that we need. But—and here is the rub—we don't know it. Be not afraid, eaters of cheese. Heavenly food is available everywhere for everyone. Heavenly food is the shelter of being enough where you are. It is the absence of need. It is a food we enjoy bodily and after our body goes from us.

The genuinely spiritual nature of our shelter has to confront some arguments against the superiority of heavenly food. One is named Rwanda. The other Bosnia. A third Springfield. Maybe you couldn't afford an anniversary party this year. Or last year. Or the year before. Or maybe you had the money but not the heart for it. But what is insufficiency but Jesus Christ unbelieved? Grace all around but none capable of seeing it. When Jesus comes into our heart, some of us at some time know what it is like to be spiritually full, spiritually fit. To have enough heavenly food that the hunger for bread or the hunger of anxiety does not invade us. When the day comes, and come it will, that we pay off our anxiety or stiff our anxiety or forget our anxiety, or jump over the fence of our anxiety, on that day watch the heavenly food. Watch it multiply into that thing we call shelter.

Shelter, salvation, shalom, security—all these words have the same root. They come from the larger meaning of peace. You can be peaceful in a tent, a hotel, a three-bedroom house—or in jail. Shelter for the spiritually homeless is first getting a spiritual home. It is to cease the worry about our physical home long enough to remember that we are but "strangers here" in the world of anxious pursuit of the additional. Our keys are in our pockets.

Evelyn Underhill, in a book called *The Life of the Spirit,* describes the law of reversed effort, that motion of the star thrower and that motion of God. The law of reversed effort, of doing the thing differently. Of the choice of the man at dawn to throw the fish back rather than to sell it. Of the choice of the housewife to stay home, happily, for the day.

Underhill showed that we can try too hard. If we try too hard, you can't get what you want. If you stop trying so hard, and let go and let God, if you struggle less desperately, you have a chance of achievement. If you struggle too desperately, you miss both the shelter and the peace that are already in your pocket. The more desperate our struggle and sense of effort, the smaller will be our success. Try hard to stop coughing and see what happens. Forget about it and see what happens. Try hard to ride a bicycle and see what happens. Forget about it and glide away. Observe any woman or any man who really wants to be invited on a date: the more desperate for a phone call, the less likely it is to come. The more nonchalant they can be about finding a life partner, the more likely they are to attract one. The law of reversed effort is the law of Christ. You can have what you can let go of. Jesus let go of life, he permitted death, and in so doing he conquered death. Martin Luther King, Jr., said it succinctly when he told some of his followers that "All they can do is kill you." What power is there in that? All they can do, said Jesus, is kill me. They can't destroy my home with my Father. Let them do what they must.

The women arriving at Jesus' grave remind me so much of my frantic searches. Anxiously they approach. Who will roll away the stone for us so we can apply the ointments? And when they got there, the stone was already rolled away! What shall we do about the stone, says worry? Reality, resurrection reality, Easter reality, tells us that all the stones are already rolled away. It is our anxiety that they are not that keeps them in place. We are in our own way. Not the stones. It is we who are in our own way, not reality.

Reality is that the stones have already been moved away. Our keys are in our pockets. We already have what we need.

God comes to me often in dreams, with angels. I'll get totally stressed out about what is expected of me, and I'll begin to worry. How am I going to do this or that, or get here or there, or ever be on time again? How am I going to find the love that my children need or congregation needs or husband needs or I need? I can win a championship with this worry sometimes. There is not a Salvation Army cot that matches this homelessness in its difficulty. Usually if I get just strange enough, just strange enough to pocket the starfish, just strange enough to require a man in my life, or just strange enough to try to stop coughing, if I get strange enough, God will come in the night, with a message. The message will be that the stone will be rolled away when you get there. Just get there. I'll deal with the stones.

My best dream lately has been a grocery store dream. I'll be pushing a cart down the aisle, looking at my watch, remembering all the people who are looking for me, who want something from me, and I'll get very tense. I'll begin to say I need to find the rice, I have to find the rice, if I don't find the rice right now, I just don't know what I'll do. Just when the worry peaks, I'll turn a corner vigorously pushing my cart, and there will be rice everywhere. Not just a little bit of rice but an entire three-star display of rice, rice so high to the ceiling that you can't see and so wide that you think the entire grocery store has gone to climb the beanstalk with Jack. I'll get the rice, and then I'll start worrying about the peanut butter, and so and and so on, all night long. I'll worry about what I don't have, I'll peak in this worry, and God will provide more than I need. This is precisely the story of my life. I worry about what I don't have, and God provides everything I need. Always has, always will. But there's no counting that I will always see it that way. The law of reversed effort. The more you worry, the less likely you are to find the rice. The less you worry, the more likely the rice is to jump into your shopping cart.

I once heard of a family who were locked in an endless battle with their adolescent daughter, who was suffering severe epilepsy. They labored endlessly to monitor her medication, to force her to get enough rest, and in many other ways afforded her absolutely no space in which to begin to struggle with her own pain, shame, and anger. The harder her parents worked to control her problem for her, the more regressed, whining, and dependent she became, and the more frequent were her seizures. Furthermore, she barraged her parents with constant infantile questions about what she could and could not do, while at the same time she continued to do the very same self-destructive things that she had requested they order her not to do.

Finally, the family went to a therapist who very wisely assessed the situation. He told the parents that there was one magical word that would help their daughter to begin to accept her illness and to control her own life and health. The magical word was *Idunno*. Every time she asked them a question about what she could and could not do, they were to say "Idunno." It was not easy for these parents to acknowledge their own impotence, but as they began to accept it, to use more and more often the magical word, their daughter began to assume more and more responsibility for her illness, her school and work career, and finally her choice of mate. Over and over again, they were reminded of the power of their magical word. They threw her back to God, these parental star throwers, they returned their child to her home in herself, not her home in them. The girl became seizure free as she relaxed into her own being and didn't have to bear the anxiety of her parents over her seizures. This may not work every time with every family; this is not Christian Science. But letting go of what we think we need is often the best route to it. The resurrection of the body may actually be the letting go of concern over it.

If we want to know spiritual shelter, we may have to let go of greed about it. We may have to live where we are, as we are, with what we have. And we may find that shelter is in our pocket.

One warning is necessary before we get too delighted with finding our keys in our pockets. Shelter is a place from which we can go out. It is not a place where we just stay. There is a subtle difference between self-sufficiency and self-satisfaction. Finally, we take our keys out of our pockets and put some direction into them.

I remember when we first moved back to Amherst. My three children had spent most of their grown life in the nine hundred square feet of a Long Island cottage. Here we were looking at the twenty-five hundred square feet of a rambling old farmhouse. The first few weeks came and went and I realized that they had set up camp in the living room. Daily more toys and blankets and pillows arrived in that small room. Daily I picked them up and put them in their rooms. Finally I asked our eldest why the children weren't living in their own rooms. After all, they finally had their own rooms and, as a card-carrying middle-class parent, I thought of this as a major life victory. Isaac told me that they couldn't find the light switches, and that they were staying put.

I respect such fear in children. And find it almost quaint. But to respect such confines in an adult is not worthy of the adult. Before you laugh too much at the children, ask yourself what form your "stuckness" takes. Gladness that there is one small room where you can be safe? One ethnicity where you can feel at home? One class or sexual orientation from which things make sense? One point on the Meyers-Briggs Scale or one point on the Enneagram? Are you glad for safety in your own living room? Or does our shelter need a jolt, a scary slide on the wall of a room we haven't yet entered, in search of the light?

As the children remind us on car trips, we are going someplace in our life with God. When, they want to know, desperately, are we going to get there? When will the shelter we know just by being be available to all the people of the world? On the Croatian and Rwandan borders, for example. That shelter will be available when those of us with too much bread learn to let go of a little of it on behalf of a larger banquet.

Our living rooms are too cramped. Too small. As that awful cliche puts it, "I can't even be safe in my own living room." Of course not. That is a ridiculous middle-class goal. Remember God's words in the psalm? Break out of the confines of your tent. Repent of your own smallness. Enlarge the limits of your home, spread wide the curtains of your tent: let out its ropes to the full and drive the pegs home...then you shall break out of your confines right and left. The keys in your pockets at home will also be your keys on the way.

Some of you may be familiar with Donald Hall's poem "String Too Short to Be Saved." Think about it for a minute. He writes the poem because he finds a box in his grandfather's attic, marked in an old hand, "String too short to be saved." But, of course, his grandfather has saved it anyway. I suppose God will do that. God will save those who have locked themselves in their living room and refuse to acknowledge their sin or take the risk of finding the light switches on the new walls. God will save the literally thousands of white people who moved out of central cities. God will save. But God will bless—and not just save—those of us who want the adventure of salvation. The breaking out of the confines of our tent. God will bless the barren and the deserted even more than God will bless those who stay scared and stuck in their own fear. Those who refuse the risk of finding the lights on the new walls.

In true sufficiency, true shelter, we link the strings. We don't make the string larger. We link the strings of our sufficiencies and our insufficiencies. Each is too short to be saved. Together they can build a safety net, a web. Together they can trap a tiger.

For the American middle class, those of us who acknowledge our spiritual homelessness, the tiger is the living room. The privatism. The barrenness of so much of our music, the stinginess and ugliness of so much of our public culture. The packaged food that has become a kind of packaging around us. The way it doesn't really matter what town you have Thanksgiving in because they all look the same anyway. That, I believe, is our suffering. That is our tent. Fast-food restaurants, minivans, and computer games, children increasingly tied to the dominant culture regardless of our best efforts to unplug them.

If the tiger is that pervasive and large, what each little string does is quite important. The way it unpackages its life, for example, unties itself from the phony bread, and attaches itself to the good bread. Some risks will be necessary to find the good bread. Our keys are in our pockets. And sometimes we will have to take them out and go somewhere with them.

THE PARADOX
OF SHELTER

"We all go on the same search looking to solve the Old Mystery. We will not, of course, ever solve it. We will climb all over it. We will finally inhabit it" (Ray Bradbury).

We have all we need where we are. We are sufficient as we are. We can be home where we are. That very sufficiency allows us to go out, to take risks, to demand more than just safety in our own living rooms, but safety in all living rooms. Even living rooms for those who don't have them. Spiritual homelessness yields a larger home. Our keys are in our pockets—and everyone else's keys are in their pockets. We simply have to find them. And finding them is not as easy as it looks. Such paradox—of ease and difficulty, of going out and coming in, of being enough and therefore demanding more—is the fat in the meat of shelter. There is more still.

As Bradbury says, it may take years to see all the facets of the mystery. The more security we find for ourselves, the more adventure we will have the capacity to seek. Being safe oddly makes us adventurous.

To be at home while traveling and to be able to skip off while at home is to know spiritual shelter. It is to live enough inside yourself that you can live outside also.

When I am at home, I yearn for travel. When I am on the road, I yearn for home. Spiritual shelter for me, and for many, is not simplicity; it is a paradox at rest.

The God of every religious faith expects these rhythms and offers them as normality, as the way it is supposed to be. God puts what we know of home inside us so that we can be home away and have a sense of away at home. God understands that we need adventure to spice our security and security to ground our adventure, often more deeply than we know. After the wilderness and the wandering comes the promised land: that is the rhythm of normal, not just spiritual, life. The more we can experience of that rhythm, the more at home we can be, near and far.

Siddhártha Gautama (the Buddha) said, "You cannot travel on the path before you have become the Path itself." Meister Eckhart said, "The Wayless Way, where the Sons [Daughters?] of God lose themselves and, at the same time, find themselves." Jack Kerouac tried to convince us that the road is the place we can be at home. And Thomas Jefferson said he would rather be sick in bed at Monticello than hale and chipper anywhere else. These apparent contradictions say more about how to find your way to a spiritual home than any straight line I have ever met.

One of the great obstacles to shelter for the spiritually homeless is our expectation that life is flat and smooth, that people like us should not experience tension but rather harmony. We should not be tossed about by tension. And yet, any of us who lives our own life and pays attention to our experience—as opposed to what we think our experience should be—knows that tension is commonplace. We call it "stress" and we think of stress as our enemy. As something that's not supposed to be, as almost wrong. "I am so stressed out," we say guiltily.

In that remark and its many modern friends, we disdain paradox. Paradox is our route to shelter: we disdain paradox at our own peril.

There is no need for guilt with regard to stress. Stress is normal, even likable. It is something we create by ourselves, for ourselves. Obviously too much stress becomes fear or anxiety. But a little stress goes a long way to keep us alive.

Stress itself is a form of spiritual shelter. We get anxious about its being a part of our life: changing our attitude about stress is what Bradbury means by "inhabiting." We will live in it, not around it. By it, not over it. Embracing, not shunning it. When we become our own way, we become sheltered. Even while traveling. Even while home. Even while experiencing the longing for home that comes with the road and the longing for the road that comes with home.

I have lived in many beautiful places: Gettysburg, Pennsylvania, where green hills rock and roll you to sleep at night; Tucson, Arizona, where the air dry-cleans your lungs every day; Philadelphia, where reminders of the simplicity of vision in which we were born as Americans compete with the contemporary ugliness and win; New Haven, where even the afternoon tea is better; Amherst, Massachusetts, that part of the Connecticut Valley where learning mixes so profoundly with living that adding chopped cookie to ice cream almost had to be pioneered; Chicago, broad shoulders carrying around democratic hopes like one-hundred-pound bags easily born; Riverhead, New York, threatened on the west by Long Islandization but still innocent of it, where the North Fork begins, diverse waters on every side, as far east as you can go and not swim; and back to Amherst, where we were married down the block from our current home, and where our firstborn was baptized. I have been at home in all these places. I still live in them even when my address is elsewhere. Some have introduced me to more wilderness; others to more promise. For each I am learning to be grateful. They are each part of the home that I carry within me. I don't carry just their good memories, but also their bad ones. Their tension is more deeply part of me over time.

The place I was born, Kingston, New York, in a Hudson Valley no one would recognize now—so ugly was it, on the one hand, and so unspoiled on the other—is the foundation of all this other homesteading activity. I have been looking for a way to get back to it since my exile at age eleven. I meet more and more children of the fifties who are trying to get back home: we were the ones who got moved around a lot, perhaps the first generation to experience moving vans as normal accessories to living.

A child in a home has all the time she needs. That memory pleases no generation more than ours: we have scheduled ourselves with the same vigor we applied to moving. I don't know which we lost first, the dailiness or the houses, but in their sheltering place we now have our schedules. We hunger for time to be in our places.

We have constant tension over lost childhood and lost childhood expectations. Then we didn't have to rush so much or order so much or make so many decisions that involved loss. As children, we see rocks as just rocks. As adults, we know rocks can also be hard places, and we often have to choose a way through them.

Shelter is not just for children. It is not just the return to a lost simplicity, but the embracing of a new complexity. Growing up does not mean we lose shelter or simplicity: rather, we gain the shelter of complexity. We begin to understand that we are many-faceted people ourselves and, as I told my husband at the beginning of these projects, in need of many fine hotels in which to reside. Our many parts need many places.

Childhood for me meant ice-skating for an entire afternoon and not giving one thought to supper, lollygagging, wasting time. Now on a good winter day, if I can get out on my skates for a quick twilight hour, I count it deep joy. Deep living in a place, the kind that comes when every chestnut you gather in the fall gets all the attention it deserves. Part of my current shelter is the loss of time for chestnuts. The loss of spring mud dancing, singing zippitydoo-dah in the puddles and not remembering that you have to be somewhere. Shelter includes the memory of there being nowhere else you are going or have to go to because you are already there. And then shelter practices that memory and lets us be where we are when we are there. Deep living in a place acknowledges that you have a home and that it is here and now, not coming there and then.

We practice the memory of timelessness in current time. That is the way: we are at home wherever we are. It just takes the practice of knowing it and remembering it. Toto may not be able to get back to Kansas, but Toto can be at home in Oz anyway.

Spiritual shelter is the capacity to travel back and forth from the puddles to the highway. It is going home to the child, every now and then, not getting stuck there, not refusing to make the appointments of the adult or to share time with a world that is older than nine, but rather knowing how to get back there, knowing who lived there, what he or she was like, what he or she felt. It is having a map home, a memory that regards home of origin so you can use it to remember who you are, in this house, this city, this day.

I remember once speaking in Kansas City and feeling quite at home there. The peace began in fear. When I got off the plane, I had a strange sensation: what if my feet weren't really on the ground? Airports bring out that fear in many of us. We are walking the wilderness of the late twentieth century, where everything looks and tastes alike, even us, and where plastic has all the victories that steel didn't have. Here we are sure that no one is genuinely human, they/we are all luggage-carrying robots. Eighty percent of the people, if polled in this wilderness, couldn't tell you what city they were in. They might not even know the import of the question.

Still, with all that air as victor over ground, with inert materials beating down on breathing ones, I did my little nesting ritual when I got to the Kansas City hotel. Clothes put away, suitcase hung, drink poured. I enjoy not telling anybody that I'm there until I'm there. (Remember *Postcards from the Edge*: "Having great time. Wish I was here"?) Then to watch out the window and check out the scene, to locate, to observe Kansas City as Kansas City, to be reminded that to many people Kansas City is Kingston. It has smells and distinctions that, lost on me, wouldn't be lost on them. What would be lost on them is Kingston, if you can imagine that!

To be at home while traveling and to be able to skip off while at home is to know spiritual shelter. It is to live enough inside yourself that you can live outside also. Shelter inhabits one paradox after another.

God's strategy in the Bible is homelessness until everybody can be at home. God is homeless. God is a refugee, an exile, an expatriate, a misfit, outcast, outsider, squatter, foreigner, clandestine, heretic, stranger, renegade, drifter, displaced person, marginal one, more likely to be found in trouble at INS than at home in a sanctuary. God is all those things we baby boomers wanted to be in the sixties. God is all the glamour of Kerouac, the Zen of motorcycle maintenance, the funk of living in a school bus when and if a bus is available. God carries a backpack. God lives alone but only as the one longing for us to return to ourselves, longing for us to return to right relationship with God.

Now that culture has refocused our desire from freedom to security in houses, now that we are terrified of homelessness, we can't understand this homeless God. We have seen enough of homelessness. We have climbed over it, pantless and nearly naked and grabbing out at us, at Penn Station on our way home from work. Exile is not nearly as attractive as it once was. Our fear of it is equally naked and grabbing and ugly. These days many of us have become desperate not to let exile reach into our mortgage. Freedom and security are so severely out of balance that they are damaging our search for spiritual shelter. We think that shelter is only security. It is not. It is also the adventure of a home away from home. It is also God's adventures in being homeless until everyone has a home.

A famous African exile now living in Paris, Breyten Breytenbach (*True Confessions of an Albino Terrorist,* 1985), has written a long story about what it has meant to him to be exiled. "If I may at this point enter a plea for exiles, I'd say that we are often enough admirable people. The courage and perseverance, the futile quest for survival of these stowaways, wetbacks, throwbacks and other illegal humans always astonish me: Tamuls sneaking with false passports over the border, Angolans surfacing in Berlin from some underground railway, Ghanaians passing themselves off for citizens from Zaire or boat people. How resilient they are. See how quickly they pick up the art of negotiating the labyrinths and warrens of different governments….The mark of the exile is that they are trying desperately to get back home. The exile is engaged with a search for home. The exile is engaged with an elsewhere that cannot be reached."

For many of us the spiritual urgency of these times is that we are engaged with an elsewhere that we cannot yet reach. We are as spiritually homeless as the people who live in Penn Station are physically homeless. God is as much with us as God is with them; God is as much with them as God is with us, waiting for all to get back home.

With God on board, mortgages occupy their proper place in the pantheon. We don't have to be so anxious about them. We may dare to be anxious about the border crossing of the Bosnians as well as our own credit cards. We may trust in God deeply enough so that "roof over our head" worries become exactly what they should already be: something that has to be dealt with, a piece of taking care of business, but not the spiritual promise or heritage with which we endow our children. Mortgages are not the ultimate but rather the penultimate problem of being a parent. Right now, American spiritual exiles are slaves to mortgages in a way that damages our freedom so thoroughly that it is hard to imagine us getting back home. The wetbacks may get there before we do.

One of the people in my congregation heard this sermon one too many times. He mows grass for a living, lots and lots of grass. How, he said, can a father working three jobs to survive, without benefits, living in the middle of an unfair recession where the rich are still making out and even the middle are in trouble, how can such a father not descend into anxiety? How can this father feel safe enough to allow his children to sense safety?

You have to believe what God says more than what the bank says. You have to believe the prophets and apostles and ancient seers said more than what you learned in grammar school in the 1950s. You have to believe that you are really safe even if you are not making yourself safe every minute of every sunny day. That is the art of spiritual survival; the art of finding spiritual shelter smack dab in the middle of exile.

No, this father did not take my recommendation to pay the bank 75 percent of what he owed it monthly and play his guitar in his extra time. Not yet. He is still too uncomfortable with the homeless God.

It is not our ability to pay our mortgages that allows us to dwell in safety. Goodness does not produce safety. Paying our bills does not produce safety. Keeping our noses clean does not produce safety. Song produces safety as much as any of its rivals. We are engaged with an elsewhere that cannot be reached. That is our home. We pay our way to it and we sing our way to it.

By talking about the homeless God, I do not mean to belittle our homes and our homesteading impulses. These are good things and our children benefit from them. We just have to be very careful not to idolize them. Furniture is not unimportant; it is just not as important as acknowledging exile.

Spiritual homelessness is a much trickier problem than physical shelter. And physical shelter is a wingding of a problem, a masterpiece of a matter; so imagine how exquisite the matter of a spiritual home becomes with such great rivals!

Scripture was obsessed with the paradox of wilderness and home, safety and freedom. Just watch the metaphors. God is our *dwelling place* for all generations. A *house* divided against itself cannot stand. I'm but a stranger here, heaven is my home. I go to prepare a place for you. In my Father's house there are many mansions.

The metaphors all travel back and forth between points of pretended opposition. They acknowledge that home is a paradox.

God provides a home on earth and in heaven. Sometimes it is like Grandma's house. Sometimes it is Daddy talking to us at night about his fears about his job and his doing so in such a way that we know that no matter what happens, we'll be with him and he trusts us and we trust him, so what else do you need? A tent will do when you have that kind of trust. Shelter is trusting that paradox can be a home.

VOCATION
AS SHELTER

Shelter is finding a place to be safe from our enemies. The myth of individualism is a direct threat to modern Americans. We need to shelter ourselves from it. Oddly, we move in with the enemy, live as though it were our friend, and assume that our own personal safety is all that matters. The enemy is defining ourselves by what job we can get.

The key way most Americans define themselves is by their jobs. Not by their field, but by their jobs. Not by the success of their union, but the success of their situation in the union. While all American historians are threatened by what happens to the field, and to the faculty union, most will act only when something happens to them. They may go to their tribe for help, but deep in their heart they will see the issue as individual. Individually caused, individually requiring solution.

The old theology of election is not dying easily: if I am doing well, it is because God likes me. If I am doing badly, or something bad happens to me, it is because God has chosen not to choose or like me. I pick on American historians not only be-

Vocation is to receive the call from God, through community, to play a part in the world. That we have reduced our parts in the world to "jobs" is more than a semantic problem.

cause I live with one but because they are the ones who know about the illusions in the American experience. That they know doesn't seem to matter: the individual frame is still their spiritual viewpoint.

Clergy like myself are not much wiser spiritually. We think of our successes and failures in parish as personal comment. Only the rare among us can look at the history of a parish and see that we are the third or fourth pastor in the century who has had similar problems with the treasurer. We may wonder why but we don't take in the wonderment. We act personally responsible anyway—despite the evidence from historical experience.

This frame of seeing life individually, by a warped theory of election, joins each American to his or her job in a troubling way. We are what we do. We are good if we have a good job and bad if we don't. Even some of us with good jobs think we need better, so hungry are our egos for affirmation.

We believe that we can offer our hard work to God at the altar and have God be pleased with us. The Bible does not encourage this sacrificial behavior; in fact, it rails against it: "I hate your solemn feasts, your silly sacrifices." According to Yahweh, you cannot use your job or your productivity to please. God refuses to be a co-conspirator in the myth of individuality.

God is not bribed by individuals or good deeds. What makes God happy—if you want to bother making God happy—is understanding God's power relative to your own. Simply put, God has it and you don't, as Job found out when he made tracks from the tribe and then wanted to please God on his own. Remember Job? He tried all these tricks. Maybe torturing Job was a very unkind way to express unconditional love. But that was the message.

Job was modern enough to want to be noticed by God. His way of getting attention was to work hard. Job thought that if he had the best fields, God would have to notice him. God refused the bribe. Job wants to be singled out, cherished, adored. He wants to be the most righteous man in Babylon. He wants to cross Alaska on a dogsled, to write the great American novel. And he wants to have this kind of life by virtue of his own integrity. His own excellence. He wants to stand out in his crowd. He's even willing to serve his crowd to do it. Job is, in fact, a very good man. He wants to be totally free and individual and also totally recognized and connected. He does not get what he wants.

Job has an inside to his head in a way that people before him did not. Job is self-conscious. He is a new march forward in history, a person who stands for a new moment in time. Before Job the Jews lived together, divided into tribes but in control of their land and their country. Then they lost the wars described in Ezekiel and were exiled to Babylon. Their land and community were gone. And so people developed the fantasy of individuality. It is not real that we can make a good life on our own, even today, but still people like Job think it is true. It is the modern fantasy.

This fantasy and its self-consciousness are our enemy as much as any foreign invader. We are colonized by it and though we are free to march about the city where it reigns, we are not free to live outside its actual walls.

What we learn from Job is that we can take the person out of the tribe but not the tribe out of the person. We still want the connection of community, the sense of belonging, the sense of being noticed by God and affirmed by God. We just offer our integrity, our jobs and our work, our various doings and plantings at the altar and yell out to a nonresponsive God, like a child at the beach, "Look at me, look at me." We start to live inside our heads as a replacement to living inside our people. The inner task of self-justification has become enormous since the fantasy of the individual became so popular.

At our best we are looking for a vocation that honors both ourselves and our tribe. At our worst we are looking for employment that will make us look good. This emphasis on appearance only underscores how important connections remain, no matter how unique we think we are.

Vocation is different from *job* and having a job. Vocation is to receive the call from God, through community, to play a part in the world. That we have reduced our parts in the world to "jobs" is more than a semantic problem. There are two ways to go at the problem behind the deflated word *job*. One is to show how the work ethic is our inheritance from Job—especially as we overdo "work." I call this work, time at the job, no work. Another is to show the underside of the work ethic, that side in which we under-do it. Americans are working too long but not too hard, for the most part. (There had to be a reason that old commercial "smoking more but enjoying it less" was so popular: perhaps because it has an echo to work experience?) What is being serviced is our anxiety, that anxiety that began with Job and hasn't even thought about stopping yet. Our economy is certainly not being serviced. Nor is our self-esteem. Nor are our communities. Nor is our productivity. We spend time at work and look like we are working very hard. But we're not doing much beyond handling our work ethic anxiety.

Vocation connects us to tribe, God, and self in a way that makes worry unnecessary. Vocation shelters. Vocation tells us we matter even if we aren't pulling down "big bucks" or don't yet have an office with a corner window. Vocation is pulling work from its extrinsic work side into its intrinsic, do-it-for-itself side. Vocation is labor for the labor; work is work for the money, the esteem, the salary, the servicing of the anxiety.

For the adult who is trying to build a spiritual home, work is one of the key building blocks. We will have to go back in time before Job to get historically ahead of him. His self-consciousness, his God-pleasing, even his hard work will have to be knocked down, punched through, gone beyond. An effort on behalf of community and pleasure and beauty will have to replace it. We work in Eden's garden when we work vocationally. My son's baseball coach operates a lathe during the day and doesn't really know what he makes! At night he works for kids and baseball. I don't need to tell you what is vocational for him. I covet lathe as vocation for him but that will take an entirely new economy, one that is many of our vocations to begin to make. Until that time, I rejoice that he has found a way for his vocational side to come out and play.

Nothing less than an economic, psychological, and cultural change will do to let vocation return and jobs disappear. There is no reason to underestimate the size of the issue for people who want the shelter of vocation and to be rid of the homelessness of most jobs. This task is enormous but it is not impossible. We do ourselves harm by not dedicating ourselves to it. If democracy means anything, it means being responsible for and to our political economy— what the Jews called "owning our own land."

Strange things have happened to people's time in the 1990s. There has been an awesome speed-up. The causes are multiple. Women going to work full time have caused voluntary organizations such as churches to scrape the bottom of the barrel for free help. It has also caused most families to lose the one who smoothed out the edges, greased the wheels, made the rest of the schedules smooth. The rare family has dinner, much less lunch, together. Each nomad is off on his or her own calendar. If a child gets sick at school, the workplace growls. If a dog has to go to a vet, extraordinary measures have to be taken. God forbid that a new appliance needs delivery or an old one needs repair. Nobody is at home. We are out, working and being owned. Putting stick by stick on the altar of sacrifice to the idolatrous Gods of job.

Beyond the dual-career family and its severe limitations of what might be called free time—most of which is devoted to domestic errands—there is the speed-up of fax and copy machines and phone mail and car phones.

Women have gone much too far in becoming like men. It is time for men to become more like women, artists at domesticity, connecting magic with common sense as a way of life. That is the cultural piece. The economic piece requires all the political savvy and organization we can muster. A WPA? Postponing college with guaranteed national service? Reducing everyone's workday from eight hours to six? (It has been done before, as in the Haymarket Affair of 1867, when workers demanded "eight hours for work, eight hours for sleep, and eight hours for what we will." Until then twelve was the standard.) The psychological piece is the willingness to see that we are not sheltered now and that we want to let ourselves know shelter.

Vocation releases us from the drumbeat of self-consciousness, now so finely in harmony with the drumbeat of economic necessity. We may even remain at our old jobs and be sheltered while there. There is nothing evil about slowly coming home, slowly regaining control over our work lives.

Shelter comes when we focus our point of view on the magnitude of grace, that we are secure if we never punch another time clock. It allows us to go back to work with a decolonized spirit, one that chooses to work rather than being chosen by work. The spiritual strategy of grace knows that grace is more important than works in the eyes of God. It takes a stand on that issue. Grace is more important than works. I may be working here all day folding metal or building cars or flipping burgers or counseling parishioners who think they own me. But what I do here is less important than who I am here. Who I am is a child chosen by God to be, not just to do. My genetic composition came together for a reason, one that makes God glad just because I am. I don't have to earn my right to a life, or to earn a living. I have a living and a life. From a person sheltered by grace rather than by works, marvelous works do emanate. That's what they do. They emanate. They ride the deep wave of grace out of the person. They aren't something his or her self-consciousness or guts has to produce.

And because other people make the same choices, we shelter each other. Vocational freedom is not something we dare do alone. One by one, our life would be snuffed out by threatened "owners" of what really is our own land and our own time. But in community, in tribe, we find vocation. And shelter.

SHELTER IS A SENSE OF PLACE

"I have traveled a good deal in Concord," said Henry David Thoreau. His uncanny ability to make us feel small never ceases. We are the people rarely satisfied in our own place. He is the man who is deeply rooted. He is our alter ego when it comes to having and owning. So satisfied with simplicity and eccentricity—or so he consistently reports—that he doesn't put down the place of his home but rather "travels" in it. Thoreau presents a pre-industrial ideal of shelter that might be useful in a post-industrial world.

For vacations, we often find ourselves going away in order to get home....Rarely do we travel deeply enough where we are to make the place we live into a home.

Especially now that we can connect to the rest of the world from our desk chairs, staying in one place and reaping its harvest have renewed appeal.

Most Americans make fun of their home towns. "Living in Kansas is a contradiction" is a popular bumper sticker. Most New Yorkers speak of North Carolina with a kind of reverence formally reserved for a good hard roll with light butter. Californians, by some reports the most place-satisfied people, vacation in Hawaii more and more.

Greener pastures are a particularly American strategy. We went west till there was no more west. We idealize the cowboy who moves on and on and on. Now as the recession has curtailed movement, we think of ourselves as stuck in one place. Before the recession most Americans moved once every five years, no doubt because they felt stuck in the place they landed.

For vacations, we often find ourselves going away in order to get home. We travel to folk cultures, unique places, small places, places that allow us to spread out—or we allow the travel industry to mimic these smaller cultures for us as we travel in our crowded jumbo jet to them.

Rarely do we travel deeply enough where we are to make the place we live into a home. Traveling here, Thoreau's strategy, is the choice that could save us from the airport. Traveling here could get us back home.

Now that multiculturalism is all the rage, place satisfaction has become an even more interesting difficulty. How can I possibly feel good about a white middle-class German ethnicity and neighborhood? Don't I have an identity that I need to borrow to be politically or psychologically acceptable? Is the white bread of mass culture—what Alice Walker calls her purple to my lavender—the only multicultural option? I think I could make it to living in one place were it not for the lure of the others, for the hope of integration, the mix of messages.

When you combine the fact that you don't want to see only one market niche of the country for the rest of your life—those of your race who make enough money to afford the homes in your neighborhood—with the green pastures pattern of solving difficulty, place satisfaction becomes both unreachable as a goal and undesirable. A possibility of shelter that is not homogeneous will be necessary for place to satisfy. We will also have to grow beyond our fear of being stuck. Something more concrete and eccentric, even simple, will have to appear as shelter. A way to live in one place so deeply that it turns the place purple? A way to live in the ticky-tacky suburbs that doesn't state the history of white people so bluntly? Or a way to live in the Philadelphia slums in a way that doesn't state the history of black people so bluntly? We will have to understand the multicultural before we can understand one place as shelter. Not all people will but Americans will: we are too far down the melting pot road now turned crockpotting and stewing to turn back.

Gary Wills says that "multiculturalism is not a deviation of the study of one's own world but a pre-condition of it. Who knows only one thing knows not even that." We appreciate each other to appreciate and understand ourselves; we appreciate and understand ourselves as a way to understand others. Neither self nor other can be appreciated alone. He means something like the cowboys mean when they light out for the territory. If all I was ever going to see in my life was Second Avenue in Kingston, I can't imagine sustaining interest in it. But if from Second Avenue, I could see the Italians two blocks over and the Ukrainians down the street, and if I could see them deeply enough to see my own Germanness in their light, imagine how much more color my life would have. Instead I got only the protective strategy of ethnicity: we ain't like them. The Italians are dirty and the Ukrainians are dumb. No wonder I felt stuck on Second Avenue, stuck in the alleged superiority of my scared culture.

The very origin of the folk culture that many of us vacation to enjoy is at home. Folk culture originates with the folk: it is local, storied, potentially deep. Instead, most middle-class white American places have actually given up our folk culture. We let it melt. We let it disappear as though denying our German origin would allow us to live better with the Naccarattos.

Worse, all we wanted to do was buy the kind of food that the settlers sold. That would make us look like we belonged in our neighborhood even if we didn't. Phony shelter has been purveyed for a long time in the United

States. If the economy is imported, so is the culture. We have let in the outsiders of McDonald's and Kentucky Fried Chicken and forgotten our old family recipes. We have all begun to look and dress alike. Our small towns and our neighborhoods, our places, are littered with cultural poverty. They are cluttered by the boxes of fast food, the same tastes, the same looks, the same stores.

I go to Lowell, Massachusetts, or Galveston, Texas, and I see the outline of a people and a culture. The buildings and the houses and the streets are absolutely stunning. On top of the outline I see billboards, garish signs, company logos, advertising everywhere. I even run into the same stores mall after mall after mall. And I grieve for all the particularity that has been lost.

To me the homogenized layer of economic culture is ugly. I hate looking at it. I will go anywhere where I don't have to see words being thrown at me. I notice that other people vacation in spots that also get them away from billboards for a while.

Or I ride the trains. All across the country the trains pull in to the old downtowns. Again you see what it looked like before it all looked the same. Lines, definitions, spaces between spaces. All that is left now is the lost elegance of city living. But at least in traveling by train you don't have to look at the new roads, the roads that exist only to support billboards and neon signs and shopping malls that all look the same, except that every now and then the anchor store switches from north to south or east to west.

What most people want in shelter is folk, not mass, culture. We could have it simply by using the keys that are in our own pockets. By eating our own family recipes.

If we can't change housing patterns, and we can't bash in all neon and all billboards or stop their spread, at least we can reinterpret the meaning of green pastures for us. We can't control the outside world as much as we can control our inside world. "Think global but act local" is a popular slogan precisely because it manages the local in the uniform.

What every pastor says to every suffering person is precisely that. We probably can't control the cancer but we can control your attitude toward it. Let's work on that.

Sinclair Lewis was not kidding about Main Street at all when he described it as small, narrow, and stupid. Small places don't have to be this way; they become this way when they trust the economic centralizers more than they trust themselves.

The spiritual lever in the politics of place is right here, in trusting ourselves more than we trust the centralizers. Weekly we battle with our kids who want only Pizza Hut pizza. I don't want to say who wins. But I know they hear us when we pick up the local pizza downtown.

Every time we appreciate someone else's food we should make our own type of food better, and teach someone younger how to do the same. Often when people get bitten by the bug of multiculturalism, they/we forget how important it is to hold our own end up, to elevate our own ethnicity to the place of appreciation.

I am so distressed by white people who wear Guatemalan shirts, Indian shoes, Chinese dresses and feel "multicultural" only to scoff at the polyester of the American "peasant." We are missing a serious beat in our spiritual poverty and our potential spiritual wealth right here.

Multiculturalism at its best is a paradox of self and other in a mutual admiration society. At its worst it is a high-class form of racism, an exoticization of the other and a put-down of ourselves.

White America not only makes exotic and primitive the racially other; we also just try to keep them out. *Nimby*ism is not just a phenomenon where I live. Across America there is a pioneering spirit that is its own debasement: now that I have my acre, I want the rest of these folks kept out of here. Once I get in, set up the restrictive zoning. We have to learn to protect our home place *and* do so from a basis richer than that of *nimby*ism. Both/and; not either/ or. Opening our small places will protect them more than building fences around them.

Open places will shelter us; closed places will lock us inside them. There is an economics of place that needs tending. If you don't want to protect your hometown or region by a hostile, defensive *nimby*ism—and if you refuse to put the place down by becoming an avid reformer of it—and if you refuse to throw away your own native ethnicity and culture—there is really only one other basis from which to love your place.

That lever is the true origin of folk culture: an interior and open capacity to generate culture and economy locally. The rest will follow. We can celebrate place as place, place as invigorated by strangers and place as invigorated by locals: people must learn to travel far and wide in their own Concords.

But we must also make our own hamburgers. The shelter of local place, local culture, local particularity is most severely damaged by outsiders with their hamburgers. They come in and remove not only money but also shelter. There needs to be an economy of place. Who knows what went first, the local economy or the local culture? Maybe they left at the same time. But to return to the benefits of real folk culture as Americans, we will have to restore real local economies. Phony ones won't do.

Instead of railing against the external enemies, our leaders should activate our inner resources. The question is not who or what we need to eliminate, but rather what we need to add and retain, steward and conserve. It is that capacity to deeply travel where we are, Thoreau's relationship to Concord, that allows living where we are to be culturally, politically, and environmentally rich. That doesn't mean keeping the outsiders out as much as getting the insiders in.

I had a phenomenal experience in Peoria, Illinois, once. The town had been put up for sale—with a town law saying that if your house was *not* for sale, you could put a sign on it. Otherwise the signs were too full of clutter. Caterpillar had moved out. There was no local economy. People felt they had to move out. Not all could make it. Those left behind set up food carts in the center of town everyday, selling food they made at home for small amounts of cash. The lunches were fabulous. Without a stage this dramatic—of local making, selling, and buying—folk culture in the United States is impossible. With it, we could all enjoy a sense of place sufficient to our longing for spiritual and real shelter.

BOYS, BURNING, AND BRIDGES

At breakfast and lunch, church and hall, tongues are clicking. The first week in August three boys burned down the oldest covered bridge in Massachusetts. We are left with what to do when our tongues stop clicking. What meaning do we make of those who were meant for good? Whose names were meant to be etched into old bridges and to remain there for centuries more, expanding with the aging wood and becoming more of themselves rather than less?

These boys saw little shelter in history. Like many generations before them in this century, they saw little use for what people had thought or done before. They felt "new."

We need a diagnosis of why children actually destroy some of what might be shelter for them. Not just bridges...but the companionship of religion or promise.

In my sixties, we burned down other kinds of bridges. "Nothing like us ever was," we announced. We seemed to believe it ourselves and some of the statement was true. No other generation had as much birth control available to it or as much money. The fact that the money faucet stopped midstream threw us for a pretty good loop. We had only been formed by money; then the money disappeared. Or, rather, instead of schools being built for us and highways being built for us and Sunday school wings being added for us, we had to tax ourselves to do these sorts of things. Even some of the real bridges collapsed, so little were the taxes we were willing to pay.

The seventies generation made a fairly clean break with the old sexual morality. The eighties generation made a fairly clean break with the traditional work ethic. In the nineties Generation X widely describes itself as despairing. Whether they actually are as despairing, one by one, as their press, surely they are being raised to hope in less future than I or my parents were. Even though one of my parents completed only the eighth grade, still he thought the world was his oyster. He would and could make good. It is the rare adolescent today who leaves adolescence with that confidence. Instead our youth wonder which of their parents' sins will kill them. Ozone or chemical pollution, vanished topsoil or population explosion, urban violence or lead paint: take your pick of enemy. They prey on both the bodies and the spirits of children today.

Sheltering those who have no innocence is different from sheltering those who do. We can make promises to innocence; lost innocence needs proof. Where will the proof of spiritual promise and spiritual shelter come from for Generation X? I fear it will have to come from themselves, from inside them. I doubt that it will come from those of us whose credibility is as lost as the ozone.

Those boys who burned down their bridge are now faced with a possible ten years in jail. Three lives may be in the process of being destroyed along with a town's memories. Lots of initials gone up in smoke. Lots of first, second, and third kisses. Lots of pretty pictures. All for the thrill of lighter oil's impact on old, dry wood.

Why? We really need to know why. We need a diagnosis of why children actually destroy some of what might be shelter for them. Not just bridges and not just history but the companionship of religion or promise. Why are so many children throwing out relationship with the "former things" on behalf of themselves and their peers?

Boys have been boys longer than that bridge had stood. One person suggested in the last century that the whole prison problem could be solved by just locking offenders up until they turned thirty, when "something" seemed to happen to calm them down. If you visit a prison today, you will see cause for a similar solution. It is young men who inhabit prisons. Young men who damage communities, young men who lose their tempers and young men who drink too much and drive too fast. Not older men so much, and rarely women.

I remember facetiously suggesting at my college that they lock up the men and let the women go free. We had to be in at midnight; they could roam. It was an odd injustice, based on the facts of who was more likely to pull up the tulips on the town common and more likely to burn down the bridges.

We can also imagine that these boys were once the apples of their parents' eyes. That some parents actually did try to shelter them. We can imagine that tears have been shed over their skinned knees. That they were like every other boy at the shore and skipped stones with great glee at their own prowess. We can also imagine that they rejected the protection offered to them in early adolescence and also that they really wanted to be able to accept it but didn't know how.

I remember once asking a boy in my youth group years ago why he had thrown the stones that broke all the windows on the new house being built next door to him. His mother was raising three children by herself. The $1500 she had to pay back for the windows took all her savings and $500 more. His response was an honest, "I don't know." He really didn't know why he had done it. The stone that should have been skipping was hurling. He really didn't know why.

Nor, I fear, do the people who burned the bridge. Whoever they are, they probably don't know what weird violence took over and let them deliberately destroy.

Those of us able to be more rational about burned bridges are left with the question of how we can prevent such "I don't know-ism." How we can deal with the needs of teens for protection they don't want, for structure they don't want, for futures they don't have, for shelter that they don't want but which we want desperately to give them.

Clearly we have social as well as personal responsibility to protect our bridges and ourselves from out-of-control young men. We need to solve this recession so that children today can have something like the future most of the rest of us were raised to expect. And we need to make divorce and fatherless homes less acceptable than they are now. Children need fathers. Young men need fathers. Fathers also need young men, if for no other reason than to prevent the kind of embarrassment that burned bridges and broken homes cause them.

We had a three-year-old child visit us last weekend. He is being raised by his mother. The child said at dinner, "The most interesting person I met this summer is my father." We all gasped—as would his father if he ever heard what the child had said. Clearly, in order for adults to shelter children, divorce has to become less acceptable. Or at least it has to become one freedom we place in our personal account book very close to sheltering our children.

When we get our own towns and our own homes back in order, then we can begin to work on the systemic issues of ozone and topsoil, chemically fast growth, and the other public threats to our children's eventual shelter. Each of these "big" things has its root in our "small" values. You don't like this wife; get another. You don't like this house; get another. Move up, move on. Doing so quickly is better than doing so patiently or slowly. You want potatoes in sixty days: grow them faster with this chemical. So what if the soil can't be used for twenty years!

Most American public behavior is rooted in American private behavior. It is as though we looked around at our public life and our land and poured kerosene on it and lit it. That's how serious has been our destruction of the safety net and the social fabric, all because we wanted something "now" instead of later. Children hear these values. They see them. They do what we do, not what we say.

What can young people do to shelter themselves? They can rebuild the bridges. Slowly. They can commit to each other, if not to us. It would help society a lot more—and cost it less—to have those three young men rebuild that bridge themselves. Forget prison. It will just ruin what is left in them to be ruined. If they did it, let them fix it. There might even be some fathers in town who might want to help.

To rebuild the broken society they have inherited so that it can shelter them, young people have a lot to do and a lot to be. They need to take over the spiritual institutions that now actively exclude them as well as rebuild the physical infrastructure that surrounds them.

Every church I know wants to know why young people don't come to church anymore. Some of that cry is phony: young people have always left church for a while in this country. But now fewer and fewer are even getting the religious preparation as youth that might allow them to return intelligently to spiritual life at a later life. Researchers tell us that youth today make a serious distinction between "spirituality" and "religion." Religion is in an institution; spirituality is pure. It is outside. Individual and quick-fix values win again. Young people live the values we teach them. The problem with shelter for children today is that our values don't shelter. They trick.

As hard as it is to find spiritual shelter in institutional "religion" today, it is that much harder to find it outside, all by yourself. What we find out there is the accompaniment of God, but not each other. The God of Christians always sends us back to each other to test the "spirits" in "fruits." In real life. Younger people today don't even have good sites for testing each other. They have a reduced institutionally based work life—is McDonald's or another conglomerate an institution or just an over-grown cell? Young people have a smaller school life—is attending a university with 20,000 other students an institution or a maze? They mistrust the law and medicine as much as they mistrust religion. Their level of aloneness is frightening.

To shelter young people, we need to teach them how to take over these institutions. For example, in the church, Bach and company need to be unseated musically. Some-one asked the difference between an organist and a terror-ist: "with the terrorist you can bargain." What we know about churches is that we actively exclude younger music. We say it is for their own good but it is not. It is selfish. (I love Bach as much as anyone but Bach has become a batterer of younger people's faith the way we have used him in the church.)

To shelter young people, we need to be able to speak about sex in different ways. Less the heavy thud of commit-ment; more the recreational aspects. Why not? Our values of sex as procreation were totally legitimate before birth control; they are not now. Children were not the biological or economic threat they are now. We destroy our credibility to shelter our children by talking sexual ethic mumbo-jumbo. If we have any chance to sacralize covenanted relationship as a sexual value—and I hope we do—it will have to be in the context of sexual honesty.

At one of the churches I care for, a conflict erupted over homosexuality. The church called a major meeting and all the recent confirmands were encouraged to come. (The "Open and Affirming" of homosexual participation in church life needed their votes.) As is typical in our denomi-nation, most of these confirmands had disappeared right after they had joined the church. One sixteen-year-old girl rose to speak. "Finally," she said, "finally, I have come back to church and found somebody talking about something important. Like sex."

To children sex is important. Music—especially their music—is important. In most churches I know, even the better ones, these languages are prohibited. If that is not a selfish withholding of spiritual shelter for children, I don't know what is.

One more fence is being built between us and our capacity to shelter children, or to be sheltered by them. It is the new language of the screen. It is not funny that sixth graders are teaching seniors computers in some American high schools. Or that my eleven-year-old son is in charge of electronics in our house. Young people need to be useful! They need to be needed. They need to be used. They need to rebuild the bridges themselves.

When all we can find to do is to click our tongue over television or hand-held games or screens, we further distance ourselves from a generation that is, for better or worse, fast on its way to being visually literate in ways that we are not. We can't expect the quality of this culture to be Enlightenment level: thirty years after Gutenberg, great books weren't being written either. We also have to watch, if we are Protestant, our Roman Catholic prejudice. The culture before we became so book- and print-oriented, so "plain," so verbal, was a beautiful image culture. A Catholic culture, one full of pictures, not words. That young people today are heading pell-mell toward a picture world is not evil in and of itself. It's just not a place where most of us can feel at home. To simply judge it, rather than to try to understand it, is yet more prejudice against youth. We cannot be a shelter for that which we disdain.

I heard a poignant story about a grandfather who took his granddaughter to see *Snow White* at the movies. He had been looking forward for a long time to the experience. "When I was a kid, I wanted to be a dwarf!" The girl fell asleep. The grandfather was devastated. "It was too slow," she said. The same grandfather watched his son's six-minute movie. The son was a filmmaker. "It was so fast," said the older man, "it gave me a headache." The son replied, "Oh, God, here I thought it was still moving way too slow."

Slow and fast are different to different generations, raised on different screens. This is not a moral issue. Fast is bad sometimes and slow is bad sometimes; each also has the capacity for good. To shelter young people, the shelter will have to come spiritually fast. And then last a lifetime.

How to shelter young people today? Let go and let their world live. Get out of their way so they can build their own bridges, their own roofs, their own houses. Trust them. They want to be spiritually sheltered too. But they will have to do it their way.

SPIRITUAL STRATEGY

A good shelter is like a puzzle whose design you don't see till you do see it—and then you can't believe you didn't see it all the time. In the pattern there was always a house; it was a picture that required sustained looking.

First we have to see the house. To see that below the obstacles of job-ism and capitalism and homogenization—even these words sound ugly to us—there is a home for us. In spite of the other scratches in the line drawing, there is still a house.

Spiritual strategy is reflection and trust in the reflection. It is looking at our own experience. And its action stage is in pressing the point: what we can do for ourselves.

Our houses rarely achieve the art of a Monticello or the grace of a woodshed but still they are our houses, if we but see them.

With all these obstacles in the path to shelter, with all this cardboard as our social, political, and psychological bed, how dare we hope to be at home now and here? We make the dare because of what Merton describes as the hidden wholeness. We look deeper and in a more sustained way—and in that spiritual strategy, we see the pattern of home. Our strategy is to see parables where others see problems.

To see the small deeply enough that we see in it the large. But our strategy is not just parabolic. It is also strategic. It is intentionally parabolic. It is choosing one point of view over another. I once called activists people who don't just care but who care actively: spiritually sheltered people are the same. We are earnest about shelter, earnest about moving into a home. We use a strategy of sustained seeing: we know there is a house in the picture and, by God, we're going to find it.

The sustained seeing is a metaphysical strategy. One that incarnates the materials that we have used for homes, cars, split-levels, fax—and our way of having supper—while giving us a place above and below them in which to live. My Puerto Rican friend laughs at the way Americans despise politics: politics, he says, is simply living consciously in society. Jacob Needleman, in a wonderful book called *Money and the Meaning of Life,* says that "the higher is simply this world consciously experienced." We need a spiritual strategy about money, not a point of view that elevates itself over money, but rather a point of view that honors and cares deeply about money and what it means.

Likewise, people don't want just a spiritual home. Nor do they want just a material home. We want both.

Spiritual strategy recognizes the material in the spiritual and the spiritual in the material. It does so by looking deeply enough at both. I think of metaphysical strategies as porches, or as bridges, connections, places from which enough reflection is possible that action is sustainable. Spiritual strategies are metaphysical strategies in the way they fiercely pursue the meaning of cars and houses and jobs and daily living. They live as though the modern secular speedy world is a monastery, a place holy enough to require sustained reflection.

The first opening of the shelter puzzle is epistemological and hermeneutical. Just because these words reside in places called seminaries doesn't mean that they have no significance as to how we think. We think in a way that makes our jobs and our houses and our cars instruments of our own homelessness. We think big when we should think small—if we take time to think at all. We think profane when we should think holy.

The second issue is measurement. How would you know if you were homeless or not? And if you decided you were spiritually homeless, how would you know when or if you found a home?

I have a friend who every year has a miserable Christmas. The reason is that she is oppressed by baking Christmas cookies for her children. Anything less than endless baking doesn't satisfy. One year I suggested that she make a dozen cookies, take two days off in December from teaching, and each day make six dozen. She tried the idea—and it worked! She spent the holiday enjoying herself, and she enjoyed making the cookies. She made a measurement. She determined what would be enough and she achieved that enough.

Spiritual strategy is at least these two steps: reflection and measurement. The way most of us live excludes time to reflect. And if you can't reflect, you have no way to measure. In the space where front porch thinking should be, advertising and culture's commands rush in and tell you how to measure your life. Big, they pronounce, is better. And we find ourselves living that way, with that hermeneutic, and not really knowing why.

Spiritual strategy seizes an interpretive initiative and declares that it will do its own thinking and its own measurement, not alone but with trusted people on the porch, so that there is some support for those inner voices and urgencies that want to live well.

I remember listening to Connecticut Public Radio the morning of Long Island's last big hurricane. The announcer, whose voice is familiar to me, said that there was a tornado watch and a hurricane watch. And there was a coup in the Soviet Union. But—and his voice changed dramatically—don't worry. Don't worry about a thing. "I am going to have a particularly nice sonata later in the morning."

The measure of distress, hurricanes, tornados, and coups, was hardly equal to the measure of redress, one sonata, regardless of how good the sonata was. I didn't know whether to be annoyed or amused by the consolation. Frequently, as a minister, I feel exactly this way. The measure of distress rarely equals the measure of redress. The sorrow is so easy to describe, the joy so difficult.

My Long Island house looked this way to me. It was made right after the war and the builder spared every expense. No mudroom. Crummy woodwork. Permanently damp basement. I see distress everywhere. My mind can so fill with the distress that I forget to look out the windows at the white pine preserve on which the house is located. I fail to see the reasons I bought the house in the first place. One look outside can equal five hours of scraping woodwork.

As one bruised by living homeless and unprotected too long, I feel that any shelter I might find would be inadequate to make up my loss. Like many other Americans, I have joined the competition of most victimized victim. I am, in the words of a *New Yorker* "Talk of the Town," "sore" and no longer have anyone to blame but myself. That doesn't mean that I won't blame others (like the cheap builder), but, upon reflection, I realize that no redress is possible. It is time to move my agony on.

Once, in a front porch reverie, I penned these lines: "I had to fix supper for my little brother. Otherwise he wouldn't eat. I spent all my life scrambling eggs. Eggs with ketchup. Eggs with blood. Now I'm real hungry. And Mamma's gone, not dead, just gone. And Poppa's gone, not dead, just gone. And God is here, just here. Saying feed my sheep. And I told God I'm hungry. Blood, wine, ketchup, I'll take anything. God, I'm hungry. What's for breakfast?" My victim was out for a whine. But at the end she shifted her strategy. The question about breakfast makes the turn. It is the metaphysical strategy, the way, upon reflection, we have nobody to get mad at and may as well go on—and make ourselves some breakfast.

I was part of a conference in Sagreb in the former Yugoslavia, sponsored by the Bosnian Women's Center. The theme was "What can we do for ourselves?" Whenever our victim goes out for a stroll, she might want to ask herself the right question. What can we do for ourselves?

Another friend was training NGO's in Romania. When he asked the people what they were hoping for there, the people said, "We are waiting for the government...to do something right." My friend was wise enough to counsel impatience about the government and encouraged going on to the more important question, What can you do for yourselves? Spiritual strategy is reflection and trust in the reflection. It is looking at our own experience. And its action stage is in pressing the point: what we can do for ourselves.

Spiritual homes are often sonatas against the storm, ways beyond the whine. They build a lot with a little. A spiritual builder changes the scale to one where a little can go a long way. Scriptures of every kind join the better movies to make precisely this point, that a little love can cancel out a lot of hate. A little bit of effort is worth a lot of hope. The Zen way of saying the same thing is that if you save one person, it is as though you have saved the world. Mustard seeds, grains of sand, little people changing big history. Religious solutions to problems involve the tricky triumph of the small over the large. They are parabolic, small stories that, if we risk believing them, carry great power.

The spiritual strategy is not to reduce expectations but rather to enlarge them by right-sizing them. Human scale is the measurement. Thoreau said, "The youth gets together his materials to build a bridge to the moon, or perchance, a palace or temple on the earth, and at length, the middle-aged man concludes to build a wood-shed with them." From grandiose hope to small hope. Pruning yields growth. Where is the shelter in lots of people trying to build houses too big for them? Shelter is much more likely to be wood-sheds, owner-occupied.

Most religious thinkers reflect long enough to change the scale by which they measure. Tai Chi is an Eastern version of the strategy. Its principle is Wu-wei or, translated literally, the principle of not doing. Its proper meaning is to act without forcing. Which is precisely what Jesus did. He acted but he did not force. It is very much the act of moving in accordance with the dynamics of water, the bending, not the withstanding. The trees that could bend were saved in our hurricane. The trees that couldn't were not. The spirit of wu-wei is to make turns with curves instead of crick-crack angles, like water does. It is to understand that this way of water, this curvy way of water, and also of the people when we act, is a powerful way to move. Water is soft and weak but it invariably overcomes the rigid and the hard. You move with the wind and the water, not only in Tai-Chi exercises, or in following Christ, but also, if you want to live well, in the course of everyday life.

Consider this connected fluidity as the measure for home. We should live more lightly in our houses. Bill Bailey said he preferred living in his shack because he "didn't have to worry about all those extra rooms." Likewise kings should move with the people, under God. People should move with each other, under God. Act without forcing. Then the small will prove the equal of the large. Which is a beautiful definition of democracy, of how people should govern themselves. The small proves the equal of the large.

If you have a long-standing grudge against someone, and even have come to hate and fear that person, for you to do harm equal to the harm done to you will violate the created order of things. Not a tit for a tat, but a smaller justice, a fluid justice. Then you will see the lot in the little. *Shelter doesn't get even.*

There is no need to build a shelter in adult life that equals the homelessness of an earlier period. There is no need to get parents who didn't parent you to parent you. Or to locate the love that a lover stole away with him or her. You build to build, not to redress.

The failures that we have experienced, and the failures that others in not loving us well have laid upon us, have something to offer as education. They are not building blocks but rather used-up blocks. When Yeats tells us that we are "bred to a higher thing than triumph," he is showing that not only the great religions, but also the great poets, understand this matter of scale.

The measures in spiritual strategy are to right-size our lives. That may mean that less is more. And it may mean we will take enough risks that wonder will create a different kind of abundance than we thought we were headed for. Spiritual strategy gets us home a lot more quickly than any of us thought actually possible.

TRAVELING LIGHT

Shelter for the spiritually homeless uses its failures to be at home in a world such as ours to motivate itself to get home. It does not believe "it can't be done" or "you can't get there from here." Rather, shelter believes the world is built wrong: it rebuilds the world and in the process of rebuilding finds a way home.

Shelter for the spiritually homeless is the ability to live and see parabolically. To find the larger meaning in the smaller life.

Experienced travelers travel light. We know that the luggage is in our way. Spiritual homes don't need a lot of "storage" space because they don't have a lot to store.

To delve deeply enough into each moment and each community to see who and what is living, webbed, connecting there. Shelter sees a lot and travels a lot in its own "Concord."

Shelter involves our own resources, our own keys from our own pockets. It does not depend on outside funding. We fund from within. We believe long enough that we have what we need that we stop looking for the bigger house, the better job, the more astute self-help workshop. Shelter lives with our keys in our pockets.

Shelter is not without dissatisfaction. Sheltered people know that even though

91

they have found the keys to their own house, others may not have found theirs. We don't shut down just because we're home. We bleed with the others who are still stranded. We identify with refugees; we don't put them down. We don't see shelter as a personal achievement as much as a God-given grace.

There is a paradox to living a sheltered life. The paradox involves the desire we have for travel and adventure, to live beyond our comfortable Concords. Sheltered people move out from time to time into difficulty and there make a home also. Sheltered people do not assume a theory of harmony: we acknowledge difficulty as part of our home and we expect it. It is not treated as an uninvited guest but as part of normal living.

Spiritually sheltered people don't live above money or jobs or status; we live through them. For us these incarnate matters are part of the flow of grace. They matter to us, but not as much as they do to the unsheltered. We have lived with such matters long enough to give them the right size in a life that, ironically, hasn't gotten smaller because of their proportioning, but rather larger. Getting to a human scale that is right for us, for our job, our bank account, and our selves, is a major piece of sheltering ourselves.

Spiritually sheltered people live deeply in a place and also without much need for a place. We see deeply where we are; live deeply where we are, and can be delighted in a four-star hotel, or a cottage. We live parabolically in place, knowing that the more deeply we look inside a place, the more we will see there.

Spiritually sheltered people know exactly what Edith Wharton meant when she described one of her poor characters as living "beautifully" in a bird's nest precariously perched on a cliff. We know how little we need to be safe.

Creating spiritual shelter for children is our own way of clearing a path in the forest of the future for their contributions to come to us. We want to receive from children as well as give to them. Rather than being anxious about the future children face, we partner with them to create one. We keep spiritual shelter as an objective in their life even though we know they may not want it yet. We shelter those who want to run free. Through our protection they will eventually see a model of life fully sheltered, one that does not exclude either youth, their unique futures, or their adventures.

A person or family could enjoy each of these graces—parabolic and paradoxical; sheltered in job, money and place; with or without children; with or without acknowledging keys in pockets—a person could enjoy each of these graces and still not be at home spiritually. We all know ourselves well enough to know that we can squeeze the juice out of joy in more ways than have yet been discovered. We can turn grace into grind and quickly. Some of us will try to turn these graces into a program and live by their recipe. "Today I will analyze each thing that happens parabolically. I will look for its paradox...." "Today I will explore my entire small town just to see what and who is there." You can imagine the programmatic development of the graces of spiritual shelter. What is recommended here is another style of living at home. It is the style of refusing the program, the manual or self-help approach on behalf of the keys that are in everyone's pockets. It is receiving the gift of shelter that God has given each human being and becoming content to live where we are, as we are, before we move into efforts to improve ourselves.

The best way I know to get out of the way of grace is to travel lightly. A parable will give one hint as to how. There we were, two twenty-eight-year-olds in love, on the rim of the Grand Canyon on New Year's Eve, watching the sun go down and realizing that the hotel really was full. Even if it wasn't, we couldn't have afforded to sleep there. But in the first years of that first marriage, we tended to take one problem at a time. My husband had a brainstorm. "I'll bet the ranger in the bottom of the canyon is lonely, especially tonight. Let's call him and see how he would feel about some guests." The idea had merit: its desperation matched our own.

The telephone number of the canyon ranger was in the book. We dialed, explained our situation, and offered a barter of groceries packed down. Gary, the ranger, said that actually he and his very pregnant wife would love company and would especially enjoy company that brought guacamole and tortilla chips.

The hardest part of the evening was finding avocados at six p.m. We did find them and didn't mind paying the rather astronomical price. A half-hour after dusk we were on our way down. No packs, except the groceries.

Whatever hatred I have since developed for luggage must have originated that night. The freedom of moving without carrying! The beauty of the canyon unobstructed by plans to see it! Gina, Gary's wife, had come on the phone and insisted that we "bring nothing" but the chips and dips. She kept saying "we have everything."

Little did we know. After a light but uneventful passage down the curving canyon, we arrived close to midnight. It was warmer by twenty degrees in the canyon. We had gone down so quickly that we passed by the ranger's house and went as close to the Colorado river as we could get. There on that hot grassy plain at the bottom we looked up and saw several caribou, like statues, preparing for their own version of "Auld Lang Syne." One coyote actually seemed to be singing it!

During the last few minutes, as we returned to the ranger's house, we had an attack of shyness. Surely this was it; there was no other building anywhere. But what if these people were serial killers? Or strange in some other way? What would we do then? Call the park ranger?

What some people see as adventure others see as stress. The reverse is also true. The stress that night enhanced the adventure. We knocked on the door and were almost disappointed to be greeted by such normal people!

They were both about our age. Gina was eight, maybe almost nine, months pregnant. They were dressed casually.

They led us into their large cabin and served us a nice dinner. Then we played games. They apparently had every board game, pool table, and entertainment device in the world. No television down that far but there was a shortwave radio that gave all the doings on the rim. "Picked up a drunk at Sleazy's Bar, etc."

The games offered just the chance to get to know each other: now, I think, in our forties, we probably would have sat there interminably having "conversation." By the time we got to the real thing we were gamed out.

They showed us their "sports room." It was full of abandoned sports equipment. High-class hiking boots. High-class backpacks. Fancy hats. Fancier walking sticks. Three-hundred-dollar down vests. Gina commented, "People can walk in easily enough with all this stuff; they just can't walk out. That's why I told you not to bring any more stuff. I wanted to make sure you could walk out."

The next morning—which came around noon—Gina served her famous pancakes. Thin buckwheats, spread with cottage cheese alternated with orange marmalade, stacked seven high and sliced to show the stripe. "These are guaranteed to get you all the way out from here. I've done it many times." She walked us halfway up the rim and pointed out a shortcut. We did one more verse of "Auld Lang Syne" together and said good-bye.

That night was a lesson in packing lightly. A lesson in not over-arranging. A lesson about youth: walking in *is* a lot easier than walking out! Should other old acquaintances be forgot, all right. But not these. Their message was too powerful.

Luggage gets in the way of our shelter. We might have seen only a little of the canyon, or the people, or the caribou, or the lesson, if we had been burdened with backpacks and preparations. Instead we just walked. We just moved. We let happen what would happen.

Most of our lives, and certainly my own, are overplanned. Overstructured. Overcooked. We are so burdened down by our poison ivy protection that we fail to enjoy the forest floor. When we move out of control, we find a larger control. The arms of God, I would say, building a house around us.

Once, flying out of Orlando, my husband and I managed to do something ridiculous that is now part of the lore of what shelter means for us. He was parking the rental car; I was holding our one-year-old twins and chasing our three-year-old son at the drop-off point. I thought he was taking the luggage to the attendant; he thought I was doing it. We both thought the other *should* be doing it, no matter who was doing it. When we got to New York and waited for a long time and realized that our luggage was still standing at the curb in Orlando, we had a great laugh. In a more anxious mood, both of us could have turned that laugh into lesions. But that day we didn't. The vacation had taken; we could live quite well without our bags for a little while.

The same lesson, with much more profundity, occurs in the great short novel by Thomas More, *Death in Venice.* The jaded Auscenbach doesn't even begin to live his brief one month of genuine life—after every opportunity to live well had already passed him by—until his luggage is put on the wrong gondola.

I don't know how many more lessons we all need. Experienced travelers travel light. We know that the luggage is in our way. That spiritual homes don't need a lot of "storage" space because they don't have a lot to store. Or rather that they may need closets but they don't make the size, shape, or acquisition of closets a major life objective.

Traveling light allows us to be sheltered where and as we are. Spiritual shelter we carry within us; it comes as we go. It is where we are. It is a gift, not a get.

Spiritual shelter finds the keys in the pocket and is able to look around and see that the keys aren't just in our pockets. A larger shelter is there, almost the arms of God, right around us. We just needed to take the time parabolically, paradoxically to see it.